The ECLIPSE Model

The ECLIPSE Model

Teaching Self-Regulation, Executive Function, Attribution, and Sensory Awareness to Students with Asperger Syndrome, High-Functioning Autism, and Related Disorders

By Sherry A. Moyer, MSW,
NHS Human Services Inc.

Foreword by
Brenda Smith Myles, Ph.D.

© 2009 Autism Asperger Publishing Co.
P.O. Box 23173
Shawnee Mission, Kansas 66283-0173
www.asperger.net

Publisher's Cataloging-in-Publication

Moyer, Sherry A.
    The ECLIPSE model : teaching self-regulation, executive function, attribution, and sensory awareness to students with Asperger Syndrome, high-functioning autism, and related disorders / Sherry A. Moyer ; foreword by Brenda Smith Myles. -- 1st ed. -- Shawnee Mission, Kan. : Autism Asperger Pub. Co., c2009.

        p. ; cm.

        ISBN: 978-1-934575-37-6
        LCCN: 2009935430
        Includes bibliographical references.

        1. Autism spectrum disorders--Treatment. 2. Autistic children--Education--Study and teaching. 3. Asperger's syndrome--Patients--Treatment. 4. Social skills in children--Study and teaching.
5. Sensory integration dysfunction in children--Treatment.
6. Teachers of children with disabilities--Handbooks, manuals, etc.
I. Title.

RJ506.A9 M69 2009
618.92/85882--dc22   0910

This book is designed in Helvetica Neue.

Printed in the United States of America.

Acknowledgments

With a rich tradition and history spanning 40 years, NHS Human Services continues to be a leader in the field of human services. As one of the first mental health/mental retardation centers in Philadelphia, NHS, then known as the Northwest Center, opened its doors in 1968 and quickly grew to be the largest provider in the city. With a reputation for quality services, NHS has become a nationally recognized, multistate, multiservice, nonprofit provider employing 13,000 staff and serving over 50,000 adults and children every year. NHS offers a continuum of care featuring innovative programming in the areas of mental health, addictive diseases, intellectual and developmental disabilities, autism, juvenile justice, foster care and adoption, and educational and specialized services.

While its geography and services have changed and expanded over the years, NHS's mission has remained firm and committed. Today, NHS is still the safety net for people who otherwise could not afford care and who "fall between the cracks" of bureaucracy and red tape. In spite of financial challenges and dwindling public resources, NHS continues to pursue excellence in all aspects of care and treatment. Surrounding clinical professionals with the best in technology and supports, NHS is a leader in the industry and remains committed to helping people … one individual at a time.

NHS is proud of the continuum of care they have created to provide services to individuals with an autism spectrum disorder (ASD). From a single program offering community-based staff support, NHS has created a range of services for individuals regardless of their age or presenting behaviors. Responding to concerns from families about the need for additional services, NHS created the Stepping Stones Program, a day service program for children ages 3-14. That program was so successful that it has been replicated at multiple sites and in 2009 served 450 children at 19 locations.

NHS then responded to a challenge from the same parents to create educational opportunities for their children who were not successful in mainstream school settings. NHS sought out experts in the field and hired a highly trained and dedicated cadre of staff to open the first NHS Autism School in Herminie, Pennsylvania, in 2005. In September 2009, NHS opened its ninth school in Pennsylvania dedicated to young people with ASD. Over 205 students are receiving educational services utilizing curricula designed to meet their individual and specific needs.

The NHS commitment to individuals with an ASD extends into adulthood. NHS has developed day programs for adults with autism and continues to work with families to create services and opportunities that will help adults with autism live independent and productive lives. NHS has partnered with parent groups to support housing and employment options. NHS values the partnerships it has created with parents, educators, and other stakeholders and professionals. By working together to achieve common goals, much has been accomplished to develop a continuum of specialized services for individuals with an ASD. NHS continues to partner with leading experts in the field of ASD and education to create teaching models and educational approaches for young people with ASD.

When faced with the challenge to provide the best classroom experience for higher-functioning children, the NHS Autism Team found that there was no curriculum that met their unique needs. NHS sought out experts on the field and hired Sherry Moyer, who had a specific background in this area, to help in the development of a new curriculum that focused on the challenges faced by these children. This innovative, highly specialized curriculum forms the basis of this book. Parents, educators, and autism experts are unanimous in their praise for this approach. NHS is proud to be part of this effort and the very dedicated staff who work hard every day to improve the lives of children with autism … one individual at a time.

We offer special thanks:

To Sherry Moyer, for the hours of hard work put into this book and for her unfailing commitment to children with autism.

To Karen Markle, NHS vice president for Autism Services, for her vision to create a continuum of care for individuals with autism, for her tenacity to make that vision happen, and for her leadership to create a team of professionals who share that same passion and mission.

To Rayni Anderson, NHS corporate clinical director for Autism Services, who has been an integral part of the development of NHS autism programs and whose skill, commitment, and personality have helped shape this unique service system.

To Heather Plassio, NHS director of development for Autism Services, who has organized and monitored the development of NHS autism projects, including this book, and who has provided immeasurable support to the entire team on a daily basis.

To the Honorable M. Joseph Rocks, chairman and CEO of NHS Human Services, who has been a crusader on behalf of individuals with autism and their families and has shown a personal interest in every family he has met. His understanding of their problems and challenges led to the NHS vision and mission to support people with autism and provide the best in clinical care and technology to enhance their lives.

NHS Human Services Inc.

Table of Contents

Foreword

We are just beginning to understand the myriad complexities that are associated with Asperger Syndrome (AS) and high-functioning autism (HFA). With this understanding comes the acknowledgment that single interventions are insufficient to address the behavior we see. The use of singular strategies has not been effective for individuals with AS/HFA, as evidenced by their dismal rate of employment and independent living as well as generally low quality of life as adults. Further evidence is seen in difficulties with controlling behavior and problem solving – both of which can lead to challenges in school, home, community, and, ultimately, involvement with the legal system.

In order to facilitate life success for individuals with AS/HFA, who all too often have unrealized potential, it is essential to design comprehensive interventions that address the underlying characteristics of autism. In fact, it is my contention that it is *only* by addressing the autism that individuals with AS/HFA can come to lead successful and productive lives. Two comprehensive planning models, the Ziggurat Model (Aspy & Grossman, 2007) and CAPS (the Comprehensive Autism Planning System; Henry & Myles, 2007), provide the tools to structure a successful educational program for students on the autism spectrum. While these models provide the essential structure, they do not address content. Now Sherry Moyer's ECLIPSE model fills this void.

The ECLIPSE Model directly addresses four challenge areas that are not directly addressed by other curricula: self-regulation, executive function, attribution retraining, and sensory awareness. These four impact almost all activities across environments, and individuals who do not have adequate skills in these areas are unlikely to achieve their potential and a good quality of life.

The following brief descriptions further delineate the importance of self-regulation, executive function, attribution retraining, and sensory awareness.

1. *Self-regulation* – the ability to detect one's emotional state and change it to match the situation and environment; the ability to recognize and control behavior.

2. *Executive function* – the ability to organize, strategize, prioritize, and plan activities – from deciding what to wear to explaining one's rationale for an action to deciding how to carry out a long-term project.

3. *Attribution* – the ability to understand why something has happened and one's role, or lack thereof, in its occurrence; the ability to accurately analyze a situation and develop strategies/tactics/plans.

4. *Sensory awareness* – the ability to detect how one's senses perceive the environment and make decisions about how to regulate sensory input.

An analysis of these four elements reveals that they may be the *essential* skills that contribute to life success.

The activities in *The ECLIPSE Model* curriculum are easy to use and highly motivational. They are based on what we know about effective implementation of interventions for individuals with AS/HFA. *The ECLIPSE Model* can be used successfully by social workers, special educators, speech-language pathologists, occupational therapists, counselors, and psychologists in both school and clinical settings. In addition, they can be used one-on-one or in a group setting.

In a small study on the impact of *The ECLIPSE Model*, Moyer found that use of the curriculum is related to student hopefulness. That is, students completing the curriculum believe that they have the tools to be successful. At the time of this publication, a randomized controlled trial is underway to further substantiate these preliminary findings.

The ECLIPSE Model has great potential to help individuals with AS/HFA to learn the skills that they so desperately need to achieve a good quality of life. Moyer's solid empirical knowledge of the needs of individuals with AS/HFA is evident on every page. In addition, her practical experience with this population is obvious. This curriculum is one that is easily used in schools or clinical settings.

Brenda Smith Myles, Ph.D., a consultant with the Ziggurat Group, is the recipient of the 2004 Autism Society of America's Outstanding Professional Award and the 2006 Princeton Fellowship Award. She has written numerous articles and books on Asperger Syndrome and autism, including *Asperger Syndrome and Difficult Moments: Practical Solutions for Tantrums, Rage, and Meltdowns* (with Southwick) and *Asperger Syndrome and Adolescence: Practical Solutions for School Success* (with Adreon). The latter is the winner of the Autism Society of America's 2002 Outstanding Literary Work.

CHAPTER 1

The ECLIPSE Model: An Overview

Imagine for a minute the 10-year-old with an autism spectrum disorder (ASD) who discovers she left her lunch at home and now has nothing to eat at school. Such an event would quite likely leave this student frustrated and anxious as she tries to find other ways to get lunch. Students without an ASD might generate alternative solutions such as calling home to ask Mom to bring lunch or asking to borrow lunch money in the cafeteria. In order to come up with a plan, students need to stay calm and self-regulate their behaviors based on the knowledge that there is a solution to their situation. Although this seems simple enough on the surface, this is actually a series of complex neurological and cognitive processes that are well documented as being challenges for individuals with ASD. While coming up with a solution to a forgotten sack lunch is not a life-altering event, early development of such skills translates into functional problem-solving, self-advocacy, and independent living skills – all necessary for successful, fulfilling adult lives.

Herein lies one of the major features of the ECLIPSE Model. The goal of improving social competence is approached through the development of global skills such as self-regulation, executive function, and knowledge of the hidden curriculum that can be carried over to every area of functioning. It is a complement to – not a substitute for – more traditional social skills curricula that focus on specific subjects such as conversational skills or relational boundaries. **Ideally, improved global skills will lead to an improved ability to use social skills effectively and open doors for successful community experiences**. For parents and professionals supporting students with ASD, there is no goal more relevant than increasing opportunities for independence and building social competence.

When this book came to life three years ago, I was searching for an appropriate name that would reflect the intended focus of the principles and activities included in the curriculum. With the help of some folks who are much smarter than I, we arrived at Essential Cognitive Lessons to Improve Personal Social Engagement, or *The ECLIPSE Model*. Over time, the content of the curriculum has evolved to include the concepts of social competence and global skills. However, at its core *The ECLIPSE Model* will always be about how students, parents, and professionals can work together to increase opportunities for successful personal engagement by students with ASD.

In this chapter, you will find a discussion of the role of global skills and attribution for students with ASD as well as an introduction to the philosophical principles of the ECLIPSE Model. As I hope you will see throughout the book, successful use of the ECLIPSE Model depends as much on the adoption or at least tolerance of these principles, such as control vs. authority, as it does on the systematic delivery of the lesson plans. Even though you may be using this book in a classroom setting with students who are a natural group, you will also find guidelines for both formal and informal assessments of group readiness for your students. You may find that there are some students who will need extra practice using the lessons on an individual level before they are ready to join in the group setting. These assessments are also valuable for monitoring both individual and programmatic outcomes, and will be one of the many ways that you can measure the success of your students. Lastly, you will see that there is a wide selection of teacher implementation, data collection, and goal tracking tools for the ECLIPSE Model to accommodate the required level of documentation for your school, agency, or even the family lifestyle of students.

Implementation of the ECLIPSE Model can be adapted to suit the needs of the organization and the students. Whether you choose to implement the model fully or are just looking for supplementary activities for your current programming, the ECLIPSE Model can be modified accordingly. Throughout the book, you will see that the curriculum makes reference to student or students. This is meant to represent children, teens, therapeutic group members, and all others who participate in the ECLIPSE Model curriculum.

Within the ECLIPSE Model, successful social competence in its most basic form is viewed as the ability to navigate daily life consistently and effectively without causing harm to self or others. Ordering lunch, choosing an after-school activity, getting the first part-time job, or achieving academically are all examples of ordinary situations requiring social competence that does not always come naturally for those with ASD. In offering the ECLIPSE Model, the goal is to build that foundation of global skills, such as abstract thinking, shift/flexibility, attribution, self-regulation, and modulation of behaviors, and open the door to more successful social competence to everyday life.

Students with ASD and related exceptionalities have skills and abilities that allow them to study subjects in great detail, pursue special interests with great intensity, and devise new and imaginative ways of looking at the world. The challenges they face center around the skills that can "make or break" a person's success in life. In other words, it is not so much a question of not knowing enough content or technical subject matter as not knowing how to perform daily life skills and navigate the social environment.

Expressions of characteristics vary greatly among individuals with ASD. Some have significant challenges with self-regulation and organizational skills while others do well academically but struggle with anxiety and depression. For individuals with ASD, nothing is ever what it looks like on the surface. Their expectations are based on faulty assumptions about the parameters of the social framework they are negotiating at the moment. What you end up with are students who are confused about their inability to interact successfully and adults who are hard pressed to explain the behaviors they are witnessing. Let's look at an example.

Sam is a 15-year-old with ASD who likes to work after school at the local animal shelter. The last time he went to the shelter, he was not able to work in the cat room like he was used to doing. Sam ended up having to go home because he was so upset. When his mother asked him what happened, he explained that he felt like he was being punished because he couldn't be in the cat room even though he saw other people in there. What he didn't realize was that those people were employees and that on that day nobody else could go in because they had discovered a virus among the cats. Sam took the whole thing very personally because of his faulty assumptions. If he had understood the situation more accurately, he might have been able to self-regulate his behavior more effectively and do something else at the shelter that day.

Working with students with ASD is about building relationships. Inside these pages, you will find a number of reasons why we must work to remove the uncertainty of the social world for students with ASD. Starting with your everyday interactions, tolerance, consistency, and respect must be present and clearly demonstrated. If you create an environment that encourages students to take chances, practice skills, and play an active role in improving their circumstances, your students will be more likely to experience meaningful and positive changes. Battles, driven by the need for authority will be LONG, tedious, and counterproductive.

Many students with ASD have been through more than their share of disappointing life transitions at an early age. Multiple schools, therapists, medications, difficult family situations – and perhaps even hospitalizations – are not unusual events for students with ASD. It is possible to reach out and influence these youngsters positively, even in large school, behavioral, or mental health systems that are otherwise not ideally prepared to meet the demands of the population. Reading through the curriculum you will see that it doesn't require fancy equipment or exotic credentials to build trusting and productive relationships that result in long-term meaningful gains for students.

Global Skills and Their Role in Building Social Competence

Social competence can be defined as the ability to integrate skills such as abstract thinking, problem solving, and self-regulation to interact successfully in a variety of settings. It is an active process of identifying and demonstrating behaviors that match the demands of the circumstances at any given moment. The development of social competence is a complicated and lengthy process that requires a combination of time, experiences, and functional global skills. Let's look at an example.

Pam is a 13-year-old with ASD who was invited to a classmate's house for dinner. At her own house, there are so many kids that she has a difficult time sitting at the table because it is so noisy. Pam is often allowed to eat in the family room so she is doesn't get upset and disrupt dinner, so when her classmate's mother invites her to the kitchen table she is anxious about whether or not she will be able to tolerate the activity. Instead of explaining herself, she takes her plate and sits on the sofa, causing a lot of confusion and awkward feelings for her classmate's family. If Pam were more socially competent, she might have been able to explain her sensory challenges at the dinner table or ask for support in a way that would not offend the people around her.

The ECLIPSE Model emphasizes the importance of developing global skills to improve social competence. These global skills can be thought of as a human operating system very similar to the Windows® and Mac® systems we use on our computers. They help us accomplish everything else we need to do. Global skills such as executive functioning (cognitive shift, planning, abstract thinking, goal-oriented behaviors, and self-regulation), processing speed, and working memory are skills that improve functioning in more than one area of development.

More specific to the populations addressed in this book, additional global skills that are critical to social competence include theory of mind, causal attribution, and hidden curriculum. Theory of mind allows people to assess or project the thoughts, feelings, and ideas of another person, causal attribution helps us to assess our circumstances, and an understanding of the hidden curriculum helps us assess the context of the situation to generate clues for how we should behave. These topics will be explained more thoroughly in later chapters. Without effective use of these skills on a regular basis, other areas of functioning such as academic, adaptive, daily living, social, and vocational skills will be challenged.

The ECLIPSE Model and Underlying Cognitive Deficits – Creating Opportunities for Learning

When writing a behavior intervention plan, treatment plan, transition plan, or an individualized education program (IEP), it is important to identify the primary or most prominent skills the student must develop in order to achieve a given goal. Learning will occur to the best of the student's abilities if the goals accurately address underlying skill deficits.

Goals often identify a completed work product such as "completing creative writing assignments" or desired social behaviors such as "transition without incident." To address these goals effectively, we need to look at known underlying cognitive deficits such as abstract thinking, mental shifting, or self-regulating behaviors and then create opportunities for learning to develop these skills. That is, before he is able to "complete creative writing assignments" or "transition without incident," the student must have functional use of these skills. Otherwise, there will be frustration and disappointment for everyone as the student struggles to understand what is expected of him. It may even lead to restrictive behavioral measures or unnecessary changes in placement. Because the ECLIPSE Model is based on current research documenting neurological and cognitive impairments associated with ASD, its lesson plans and goals directly address the underlying skills that improve other areas of performance.

Take for example the teenager who is given to screaming profanities at adult authority figures when faced with stressful situations. While it might be an expression of frustration, screaming also indicates a clear lack of problem-solving and self-regulation skills that must be learned before the behavior will change. So in this case, if the IEP or behavior plan goal states, "John will express his emotions appropriately," it does not guarantee that John will learn the underlying skills that will keep him from getting angry in the first place. He may be introduced to a number of strategies such as asking for a break or deep breathing, which, if demonstrated correctly in the middle of the "crisis," may help to avoid inappropriate or disruptive behaviors. Given that deficits in self-regulation or "modulation of affect, motivation, and arousal" is a diagnostic criterion for Asperger Syndrome, that is a lot to ask. If this goal can be reframed to read "John will learn to self-regulate his behavior through the use of a modulation scale," it becomes clear that, over time, he will be given the opportunity develop the ability to self-regulate or modulate his behavior, stay relatively calm, and replace his need to use profanity with more appropriate behaviors.

Let's look at a few more examples of goals that can be reframed to address underlying neurological or cognitive deficits and create more successful opportunities for learning.

Original Goal	Behaviors of Concern	Underlying Skill Deficit	Reframed Goal
"Will develop flexibility and make appropriate decisions when dealing with unpredictable events."	Behaving appropriately when presented with unplanned events.	Problem solving, abstract thinking, shift, self-regulation and modulation of behaviors, which are too many to address in one goal.	One possibility might be: "Will improve problem-solving skills through direct instruction in abstract thinking."
"Will demonstrate improved social and play skills in order to effectively interact and participate in age-appropriate opportunities for play."	Interacting successfully with classmates or peers.	Reciprocity or turn taking, self-regulation, causal attribution, theory of mind, abstract thinking, which are also too many to address in one goal.	One possibility might be: "Will learn to more accurately assess social circumstances using the three parameters of attribution retraining."
"Will maintain part-time employment in the community."	Developing vocational skills during the transition process.	Planning, abstract thinking, self-regulating and modulation of behaviors, shift/mental flexibility, self-awareness, self-monitoring performance, using schedules and hidden curriculum – just to start. Also WAY too many for one goal.	One possibility might be: "Will learn to identify the unwritten social expectations or hidden curriculum of the work environment."

Remember that each of the goals can be used in an IEP or treatment plan based on the student's current programming. Only the goal is included in the ECLIPSE Model. Criteria for measurement, such as "8 out of 10 times weekly for 6 consecutive weeks," must be added by each student's team or primary educator, as appropriate.

It is important to remember that in many cases, the fundamental skill deficits being addressed in the ECLIPSE Model have been part of students' profiles for their entire lives. In other words, it is unreasonable to expect immediate and permanent change when the young person we are supporting is attempting to change a lifetime of skills and behaviors. Therefore, it is our job as parents and professionals to create an environment where specific timelines are not the deciding factor for how much progress any student can make.

Control Versus Authority – Using Relationships to Build Progress

If it were possible to take on the perspective of an individual with an ASD for a moment, we might see just how unpredictable, isolating, and challenging their "typical" world can be. This population of learners is characterized by significant challenges with flexibility of thought and behaviors, as well as a variety of cognitive deficits that stack the deck against effective or positive social interactions. Knowing this, the adults who support these students must present themselves and the environment in a way that allows for meaningful or functional understanding of the world.

Having control of the circumstances, for the purpose of this curriculum, allows us to manage the parameters of the environment. This means that we can manage the curriculum materials, number of opportunities for learning, level of tolerance for behaviors, and the way information is being presented, all in a way that we have thought about and determined ahead of time.

Authority, on the other hand, is a means of behavior management that adults default to when they lose control of the environment. The concept of authority is a social construct that serves a vital function in many environments. However, since individuals with ASD do not recognize or understand social positioning naturally, reliance on authority instead of maintaining control of the situation is a fruitless and frustrating approach. The old adage that "Because I said so" is enough of an answer is a good example of the use of authority to try to manage the behavior of any student. While it might be effective for some students, an individual with ASD might not understand the implied importance of that statement. You might get an answer like "So what?" or "That doesn't make sense." While this appears to be a very rude or disrespectful response to an adult, in most cases it is not intended that way. Instead, the person with ASD likely needs a more concrete or factual answer in order to comply with the request. Here is an example.

Authority: During a fire drill a teacher in the hallway sharply says to a student "Be quiet." This may work, but it may also cause the student with ASD to escalate because he thinks the teacher is "mean," "stupid," or may be "picking on" her.

Control: "The rule is that there is no talking during a fire drill." This explanation provides information that helps the student with ASD process and problem solve her way through the situation. It doesn't guarantee compliance, but it is much more likely to prevent behavioral escalations or time-consuming disruptions.

Here are further examples that illustrate the difference between control and authority.

Control vs. Authority

Situation	Authority	How to Take Control of the Situation
David, a 6-year-old student with ASD, is consistently disruptive during handwriting. He tries to hide under his desk, rocking back and forth loudly saying, "I'm not coming out!" Instead of offering David the choice of a shorter assignment, keyboarding, or having an aide serve as a scribe, the teacher calls for support from administrators. The principal and a guidance counselor come to the room, physically remove David from underneath the desk, and escort him to a "quiet room" where he proceeds to have a complete meltdown. David is not able to return to class for 40 minutes.	David's teacher opted for the use of administrative personnel to carry out a behavioral solution that does not leave David with any opportunity to try to problem solve, self-regulate his behavior, or maintain his dignity. Using this approach, no learning has taken place, and the behavior pattern is likely to occur again!	David demonstrates a pattern of disruptive behaviors to avoid an activity that is unpleasant for him. His teacher could have presented some alternatives to David, thereby avoiding a disruption that is time consuming and traumatizing to David.
Cindy is a teen with ASD who suffers from clinically significant anxiety. She is afraid to ride the bus to school, so her mother drives her. But sometimes Cindy has difficulty leaving the car or staying in the building once she gets there. On one occasion, Cindy made it inside the school but started to panic and demanded that her mother be called because she "couldn't do this." Because she was not able to calm herself, she attempted to run outside to catch her mother. In the process she stepped on the principal's foot and pushed him out of the way. The principal called Cindy's mother and the state police. Cindy was given a choice between going with the police or being admitted to a local mental health facility. Cindy and her mom chose the mental health facility, and Cindy ended up spending a week in the hospital.	The principal did not make any attempt to diffuse the situation or reduce Cindy's anxiety before she felt the need to leave the building. As a result, Cindy experienced a major trauma by being hospitalized.	The principal and the rest of Cindy's team members could have taken proactive steps to reduce Cindy's anxiety. They could have created a behavior plan that would give Cindy extra time to come into the building in a quiet area or have moved her to a smaller class so that she was not so overwhelmed. While this approach would probably be helpful for Cindy, more than one intervention might be necessary to relieve her anxiety and improve her behaviors.

Assessing Group Readiness and Progress

Not every student has the tolerance necessary to function in a group environment. For such students, the lesson plans in the ECLIPSE Model may be used individually until the student has progressed sufficiently to join the group. The most important thing to remember is that each student's needs should be considered individually and accommodated as much as possible.

If you are a teacher in a classroom, your group composition will be dictated by the students in your class. However, if you are aware of one or more students who need additional individual work before they would be comfortable and successful working with the rest of the class in a group environment, you can adjust the order of the lessons to accommodate their individual needs.

Informal

If you choose to take a more informal route to assessing group readiness, be sure to include students whose primary diagnoses are an ASD, nonverbal learning disability, attention deficit-hyperactivity disorder (ADHD), and anyone else who has sufficient communication skills to participate in the activities. Because the skills in the ECLIPSE Model are representative of global skills that everyone has, there are many students who will benefit.

A Cautionary Note: Diagnostic labels are often misused, so don't be caught in the trap of "group entrance by diagnostic label."

Another informal means of assessing group readiness would be to use the five Group Readiness Questions on pages 12-13. Each question targets a curriculum component and gives you some idea of the student's current global skill functioning. Be sure to note whether or not the student gives a reasonable answer to each question that includes sufficient detail and the appropriate context or circumstances. This is a very subjective method, but if you are satisfied that the student is able to comprehend the question and give a well-defined answer, she may be appropriate for the group. Answers to these questions should never be used as the sole indicator of group readiness. However, if the student struggles substantially with answers, it probably is a reasonable indicator that she would benefit from individual skill development activities before entering the group.

Group Readiness Questions

1. **Tell me about a time when somebody made you angry. (attribution)**
    Find out what happened, and ask the student to explain why the other person behaved the way described. You are likely to find that the student is not able to convey the situation in a way that makes sense or that he misunderstood the intentions of the other person.

    Example:
    Group Leader: Tell me about a time when somebody made you angry.
    Student: My sister and I got into a fight because I couldn't find my favorite Transformer.
    Group Leader: Why did you fight with your sister about that?
    Student: Because she hid it on purpose to make me angry.

2. **Can you describe what a city should look like? How about the country? (cognitive skill building, abstract thinking, and shift/flexibility)**
    You are looking for the amount of detail and how well the student can construct the concept of a city or country. This is a pretty concrete concept, so it may not be challenging for all of the students. Asking the two questions together, however, requires the student to form two distinctly different concepts and shift or move between them in order to come up with an answer. If you find that your student can provide an appropriate answer to these questions, you may want to try a more abstract concept with a question like "What makes somebody your friend?" Don't be surprised if you get a very limited answer like the example below.

    Example:
    Group Leader: What makes somebody your friend?
    Student: A friend is somebody who will sit on the bus with me.
    Group Leader: Is that it?
    Student: Well, my friend Dominique sits on the bus with me, and we talk about cars, too.

3. **Tell me how you would behave if you were in a restaurant like McDonald's. How about a fancier restaurant like Outback Steakhouse or Ruby Tuesday (feel free to substitute another restaurant in your area as long as it is not fast food). (social skill building, hidden curriculum)**
    You are trying to determine whether or not the student has any understanding of the "unwritten rules" or expectations for behavior in different types of situations or places. Individuals with ASD often do not pick up on the clues from the environment that determine how we should behave. In this example, behavior in a fast food restaurant would be much more informal, loud, and active than in a sit-down restaurant, which is more formal.

Example:

Group Leader: How would you behave in McDonald's?

Student: I would probably eat my burger. I can also talk on my cell phone or yell to my friends when they come in; nobody will care.

Group Leader: Would you do the same thing at a fancy restaurant?

Student: Sure, what's the difference?

4. **What kinds of situations make you physically uncomfortable? Loud noises? Bright lights? Being too hot or too cold? Bad smells? (sensory awareness)**

The answers will be different for everyone. There is growing evidence that individuals with ASD have sensory processing challenges in one or more of the senses. It is important to help students understand that the way their body responds to the environment will influence the way they behave.

Example:

Group Leader: What kinds of situations make you physically uncomfortable? How about when you are too hot, there are lots of bright lights in a room, or you are presented with types of food that you don't like to eat?

Student: Well, I really hate being in the cafeteria because it STINKS, and it is too noisy.

Group Leader: How do you deal with that?

Student: Sometimes I am O.K. because I concentrate on eating in a hurry, but then I hate to wait for everyone. At other times, it gets so bad that I have to leave and I don't eat. I just ask to go to the nurse or the counselor.

5. **Can you give me an example of something that upsets you? How do you know when you are getting upset? Does your behavior change when you get upset? Can you ignore things that upset you? (self-regulation, modulation of behaviors)**

This question is designed to help identify how well students recognize that their behavior is escalating and how well they can control their reactions. Self-regulation and modulation of behavior is one global skill that must be functional if the others are to develop.

Example:

Group Leader: Give me an example of something that doesn't upset you. How about something that makes you crazy? Can you ignore things that upset you?

Student: I guess I don't mind doing my chores. I hate it when I am late for school and work. I have a really hard time ignoring stuff that bothers me. I can't stop thinking about it, so it takes a long time to get over it.

Formal

The formal route of assessing group readiness involves using standardized assessments that teachers, parents, and others complete and/or student surveys and standardized attribution questionnaires. Two standardized tests and one attribution questionnaire most closely match the targeted skills and focus of the ECLIPSE Model. They can be used to measure more than 20 areas of functioning, target areas of significant impairment, and accumulate substantial amounts of information about each student.

> NOTE: If you are using the ECLIPSE Model curriculum as part of a student's required special education services, the student's school district may require standardized testing.

- **Behavior Rating Inventory of Executive Function or BRIEF** (Gioia, Isquith, Guy, & Kenworthy, 2000): Scales include inhibition, shift, emotional control, working memory, plan/organize, organization of materials and initiation. These are completed by the teacher and the parent; for older students, there is a self-rating scale.

- **Behavior Assessment System for Students Second Edition or BASC 2** (Reynolds & Kamphaus, 2004): Scales include adaptability, activities of daily living, depression, conduct problems, attention, anxiety, leadership, functional communication, hyperactivity, and withdrawal.

- **Children's Attributional Style Questionnaire (CASQ)** (Kaslow, Tanenbaum, Seligman, Abramson, & Alloy, 1995): This is one of the most widely used assessments of attribution style and the model from which most others are designed. It consists of a series of 48 questions that are completed by the student, usually within 10-15 minutes. The CASQ measures the student's natural patterns of attributing the stability, controllability, internality or externality and their level of positivity or negativity. (See Chapter 2 for more detailed information on attribution.)

Your choice of method of assessing group readiness will depend on time and resources. Not everyone is able to purchase or perform formal testing. However, by using the record-keeping materials in this book, you will be able to monitor student progress and make programming changes when necessary. One last important note: Never be afraid to make a change in placement if your student and the data are pointing in that direction. There is no substitute for listening to students, especially when establishing relationships. If they are frustrated or refuse to participate because of difficulty or boredom, you may want to re-evaluate your original decision. The only real mistake you can make is to ignore the facts and arbitrarily decide your student's fate. If the group is not productive or the other students are not learning because of one student's challenges, your data should indicate that it is time to make a change. Your goal is to apply these facts in a thoughtful, sensitive manner in order to maximize the student's progress and create an effective group atmosphere.

Getting Started Using the ECLIPSE Model

The ECLIPSE Model group profile charts give you some general guidelines for student profiles and when to introduce specific topic areas. Introduction of topic areas or lesson plans should be specific to your student's needs; however, the charts show the intended progression of skill development that the ECLIPSE Model curriculum employs. Here is a brief case study to help illustrate the use of the charts.

There are seven students in Mrs. James' fourth-grade class. Many of the students struggle with reading skills and require multiple prompts to stay on task throughout their day, so she chooses the profile chart for younger students, ages 6-11 years. She has the group begin with the self-regulation lessons in Step 1. Mrs. James slowly introduces the lessons as she sees evidence of her students' progress; however, there is one student in the class who is not able to keep up with the others. She suspects that he is not comprehending the activities as well as the others, so she offers him extra practice using the materials individually and makes modifications to the lessons so that they are more visual. After a few weeks of the individual support, the student is able to engage effectively with the rest of the class, and they move on through the rest of the steps on the chart together.

Model Group Profile Charts

STEP 4

Continue Daily Use of Modified 3-Point Chart, Self-Awareness Builders and Independence Journals. Add Modified Hidden Curriculum Introduction and Hidden Curriculum Diary. Periodically Review Previous Lessons.

Lessons in This Group Profile May Be Used Individually for Skill Building Prior to Group Participation

Younger: Ages 6-11 years

Reading Comprehension Must Fall More Than 1 Year Below Grade Level.

Is Not Able to Complete Any Seatwork Independently Without Multiple Prompts or 1-1 Supervision.

Can Only Give Limited Explanations for Events.

Cannot Answer More Than 1 or 2 of the 5 Group Readiness Questions.

STEP 1

Self-Regulation, Keeping a Balance, Getting to Know Ourselves (Make Modifications Using Pictures) **USE MODIFIED 3-POINT CHART.**

STEP 3

Continue Daily Use of Modified 3-Point Chart, Self-Awareness Builders, and Independence Journals. Add Modified Cognitive Shift and Flexibility. Periodically Review Previous Lessons.

STEP 2

Continue Daily Use of Modified 3-Point Chart, Self-Awareness Using Primarily Sensory Lessons, Modified Self-Awareness Builders, and Independence Journals. Periodically Review Previous Lessons.

STEP 4

Continue Daily Use of 3- or 5-Point Chart, Personal Modulation Trackers, Personal Goal Trackers, Self-Awareness Builders, and Independence Journals. Add Hidden Curriculum and Social Problem Solving Abstract Lessons. Periodically Review Previous Lessons.

ECLIPSE Model Group Profile

Younger: Ages 6-11 years

Reading Comprehension Must Fall Within 1 Year of Grade Level or Higher.

Able to Complete Some Seatwork Independently.

Can Give Basic Explanations for Events.

Can Provide Answers to at Least 3 of the 5 Group Readiness Questions.

STEP 1

All Self-Regulation Lessons, Introduce Attribution/Assessing Your Circumstances Concrete Lessons. **USE 3- or 5-POINT CHART.**

STEP 3

Continue Daily Use of 3- or 5-Point Chart, Personal, Modulation Tracker, Personal Goal Trackers, Self-Awareness Builders, and Independence Journals. Add Cognitive Shift and Flexibility, and Abstract Thinking Lessons. Periodically Review. Previous Lessons

STEP 2

Continue Daily Use of 3- or 5-Point Chart. Add Personal Modulation Tracker and Personal Goal Trackers, Self-Awareness Using Primarily Sensory Lessons, Expectations Lesson, Theory of Mind Lessons, Self-Awareness Builders, and Independence Journals.

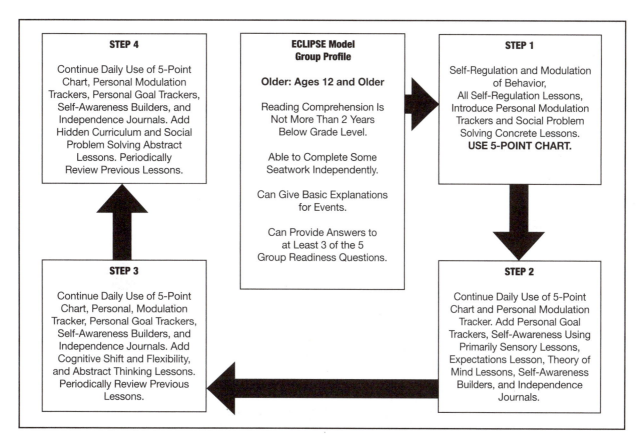

STEP 4

Continue Daily Use of 5-Point Chart, Personal Modulation Trackers, Personal Goal Trackers, Self-Awareness Builders, and Independence Journals. Add Hidden Curriculum and Social Problem Solving Abstract Lessons. Periodically Review Previous Lessons.

**ECLIPSE Model
Group Profile**

Older: Ages 12 and Older

Reading Comprehension Is Not More Than 2 Years Below Grade Level.

Able to Complete Some Seatwork Independently.

Can Give Basic Explanations for Events.

Can Provide Answers to at Least 3 of the 5 Group Readiness Questions.

STEP 1

Self-Regulation and Modulation of Behavior, All Self-Regulation Lessons, Introduce Personal Modulation Trackers and Social Problem Solving Concrete Lessons. **USE 5-POINT CHART.**

STEP 3

Continue Daily Use of 5-Point Chart, Personal, Modulation Tracker, Personal Goal Trackers, Self-Awareness Builders, and Independence Journals. Add Cognitive Shift and Flexibility, and Abstract Thinking Lessons. Periodically Review Previous Lessons.

STEP 2

Continue Daily Use of 5-Point Chart and Personal Modulation Tracker. Add Personal Goal Trackers, Self-Awareness Using Primarily Sensory Lessons, Expectations Lesson, Theory of Mind Lessons, Self-Awareness Builders, and Independence Journals.

Unique Features of the ECLIPSE Model

Magic Statements

Magic Statements are included in the ECLIPSE Model for use at those pivotal moments when students are struggling and behaviors escalate. They allow adults to maintain control in a non-threatening, tolerant way. Using Magic Statements is a bit of a departure from traditional approaches to behavior management during periods of escalation in that you are actively addressing the student during a behavior disturbance, which is not encouraged by some professionals.

If the goal is to increase opportunities for learning and build social competence, using the five Magic Statements will decrease the amount of time spent on "damage control" and reduce the overall disruption to the class or group environment by:

1. Validating the student's right to his feelings.
2. Acknowledging the need for extra time to process information and complete the activity.
3. Modeling tolerance and building trust.
4. Providing a means of maintaining the student's dignity.
5. Encouraging more adaptive problem-solving skills instead of allowing the situation to escalate beyond the student's level of self-control.

Magic Statements

1. What can I do to help you make things better?
2. Do you need a little more time to answer/finish what you were doing?
3. I will help you figure this out when you are calm enough to problem solve.
4. I understand that you are upset.
5. You have a right to your feelings.

Embed Factors

On each of the lesson plans as well as the ECLIPSE Model Implementation Record (pages 202-205), you will find what is referred to as the Embed Factor. This number represents the number of times you can reasonably expect that you will need to review a lesson before students are able to embed the skill as a regular part of their day, based on its level of difficulty. Some students may achieve their goals prior to reaching the Embed Factor. Others need more support before becoming proficient at the targeted skill. The range of the Embed Factor is 1-10 review trials, and is a general indicator of the complexity or importance of a given skill. Thus, it is safe to assume that the higher the Embed Factor, the more critical is the need for successful acquisition and performance of the skill in question.

You will be able to record the date when you introduced the lesson and the date for up to 10 review trials on the Implementation Record. Review trials do not have to be a repeat of the complete presentation of the lesson. However, they should take enough time to be meaningful for the students. Depending on how often your group meets, successful embedding of a skill can take up to a few months.

The Modulation Chart

Another critical component of the ECLIPSE Model is the 3- or 5-point Modulation Chart featured in Chapter 6 on self regulation. The Modulation Chart provides students with a concrete, visual support in the form of a numeric system for determining how serious ordinary situations are and how to respond to them in a balanced way instead of over-reacting. When taught in combination with attribution, the two become powerful tools for students with ASD who are struggling to gain social competence.

Because the Modulation Chart is so integral to the ECLIPSE Model, it is one of the first lessons introduced in the group profile charts (see pages 16-17) and referenced for use in many of the other lessons as well. Once completed, it should be viewed as a proactive strategy for giving students with ASD an opportunity to learn to self-regulate their behavior. The more often it is used, the more progress the students will see. Think of the Modulation Chart as a regular part of the student's daily routine and behavior interventions and, therefore, make sure it is accessible on a continuing basis.

The X + 10 Relevance Rule

One of the questions that parents and professionals must ask themselves when creating treatment plans, transition plans, or IEPs is: "Will this skill be relevant, or support development of other relevant skills, 10 years from now?" This is the heart of the X + 10 Relevance Rule. By identifying a skill or behavior for inclusion as a goal in a student's programming, you are committing precious time and resources to ensure it is successfully achieved. Knowing how to stand in line quietly, write in cursive (except for a signature), or making at least three new friends – common student objectives – are all skills that are useful, but they will either develop over time as a result of improved global skills, become irrelevant, or be satisfied in other ways as an adult.

The X + 10 Relevance Rule is meant to point out the need to prioritize our goal selection and weed out the clutter of numerous goals that may or may not improve social competence as adults. Including excessive numbers of goals will be cumbersome for team members to manage, and virtually impossible for the student with ASD to comprehend or remember.

Continuous, Ongoing, Perpetual, and Never-Ending Activities!

Some activities are so useful that you just can't stop doing them. Obvious examples include eating and sleeping, but you could also think about things like personal grooming or learning new skills. The four activities in this section – Independence Journals, Reality Check, Self-Awareness Builders, and Strategic Bombs – are so useful to individuals with ASD that they should be seen as Continuous, Ongoing, Perpetual, and NEVER-Ending. In other words, the more consistently they are included in their daily schedule, the more your students will benefit from them. Here is how they are used within the ECLIPSE Model.

Independence Journals

Independence Journals are designed to give students an opportunity to integrate many of the skills they are developing through the ECLIPSE curriculum into everyday activities. Each student will need a personal journal. To help foster a willingness to try new things, complete tasks independently, and build self-esteem, students should be instructed to try one new task or activity independently each week, or between group sessions. Tasks can be as simple as making their own breakfast, feeding family pets, or getting ready for school. For students who show more independence, suggest new things like reading a newspaper or cleaning their room. Remind students that if they take trips or go to special places, they should try something new while they are gone. New things can happen anywhere, so the possibilities are endless! For students who are challenged by writing, allow them to draw a picture of what they did or dictate their answers.

By incorporating the Independence Journals into your ECLIPSE Model programming, you will further encourage students to work on all of the global skills included. For example, if a student tried making lunch for himself, he would have to form abstract ideas about what food to make, shift from one idea to another while going through the steps of making lunch, and self-regulate behaviors to finish making the lunch successfully.

At the beginning of a group session, devote the first 10 minutes to students writing or drawing pictures in their journals about the new thing that they did independently during the previous week. When everybody has completed their Independence Journal entries, ask them to take turns sharing what they did. It is a nice way to "warm up" the group, get to know more about each other, and share things they are comfortable talking about.

Reality Checks

This activity is the ECLIPSE Model's version of "Current Events." Because individuals with ASD in general have limited areas of interest, it is a great idea to support growth of an understanding of "daily life." You can start the process by sharing an article. Topics can include traditional current event items such as news and sports, or cover a student's special interest area, as long as it is something recent. Since one of the goals of this activity is to help broaden the range of interests of your students, remind them that they can report on their special interests more than once, as long as there has been a new or recent finding that adds something different to the discussion.

If you find that students struggle, write down specific but fun topics that they should look for when deciding what to read and talk about, such as the environment, hurricanes, earth quakes or volcanoes, foreign countries, new books or movies, and scientific breakthroughs.

Every time you meet, spend a few minutes on the Reality Check. Be sure to prepare a back-up item or two each week, in case students forget or are stuck for ideas. The activity should be short, fun, and informative. Students will benefit from developing new interests, gaining new knowledge, and expressing their interests in small-group settings.

Self-Awareness Builders

Close each session with a Self-Awareness Builder. This is a great form of wrapping up the session or ending the school day because the group will be discussing things that they have learned or observed about themselves during the lesson's activities. After the group progresses to using their Personal Goal Tracker sheets (see pages 217-218), take a vote to see if they would like to share the progress they have made on their individual goals. To add a twist to this activity, ask the group if they would like to make a weekly list of what they discovered about themselves on the board or on a poster.

This is a time for reflection, which is not easy for an individual with ASD. Encourage acceptance and tolerance so students will build enough trust to share their thoughts. Explain to the group that everyone is entitled to his or her own opinion and that there are no right or wrong answers to this activity. You may even want to create a group rule that addresses this. Ask students to talk about at least one thing that they learned, observed, or enjoyed while they were at group that day. It is perfectly acceptable to talk about activities that they did not like.

Depending on the size of the group, plan 10-15 minutes to complete this activity. Feel free to be creative with the format as long as you reinforce the idea that students are building an awareness of their preferences, interests, and needs while doing the activity. Sometimes you may want to have the students volunteer to share their ideas, draw pictures, or even have a day where they are free to "fuss and carry on" without consequences about things found to be challenging.

 # Strategic Bombs

Strategic Bombs are meant to help students realize that sometimes the strategies they choose to deal with challenging circumstances are not the most socially appropriate or effective. The bombs – Perspective Pickle, Perseveration Station, and Smart Card – represent the more common underlying causes of frustration or misunderstanding during social interactions.

The **Perspective Pickle** illustrates the idea of theory of mind, or rather the lack thereof. At those moments when a student is struggling with another person and his explanation of the situation indicates that he has made an incorrect assumption of what the other person was thinking or intending, he is in a Perspective Pickle. Because people with ASD generally are not able to gauge others'

Perspective Pickle

You are interacting with others and have determined that you thoroughly and accurately understand their thoughts, feelings, and intentions. You are ready to act but find no success.

thoughts and intentions with any degree of consistency or accuracy, their interactions often end negatively even though they never intended for it to be that way.

Adam has always been taught to make eye contact and greet people he sees because it is polite and respectful. While walking in the hallway one day, he sees another student so he says hello and looks directly at her. She does not respond to him and keeps walking, so Adam gets upset and complains to the teacher that the student "ignored him" and "must hate him." After the teacher talks with both students, Adam discovers that the other student was busy thinking about a report she was giving in her next class and just didn't notice him. The teacher and Adam talk about how he could have saved himself a lot of emotional upset if he had asked what the student was doing before he assumed she was ignoring him.

A ticket to **Perseveration Station** (also the title of a song by Jeanne Lyons that may be found at http://www.bitlink.com/jeannelyons/samples.html) is appropriate for those situations when students are engrossed in an activity and don't feel they have had enough time to learn or do everything they wanted to do. Let's look at an example.

ADMIT ONE
GOOD FOR ONE-WAY TRIP

P

PERSEVERATION
STATION

At the absolute worst moment when you are desperate for ideas and want to do the right thing, your brain completely freezes. You have no choice but to insist that you are right or refuse to move on to the next activity.

Ricky is at his first job at the local garden center. He and his parents thought it would be a good idea for him to work there because he has always loved plants and helping with his family's gardens at home. His job is to water the plants that are kept behind the building and to bring those plants to the front of the store when it needs to be restocked.

One afternoon Ricky's supervisor asked for a cart of plants to be brought to the front, but Ricky was busy moving the plants in the back to be sure that each type got the optimal amount of sun and wouldn't dry out before they were sold. After about 20 minutes had gone by, Ricky's supervisor came back and asked why he hadn't brought the plants to the front yet. Ricky replied that he thought it was more important to finish his reorganizing and that he would bring the plants when he was done.

What Ricky didn't do was explain why he was reorganizing or what the benefits of the reorganization might be, so his supervisor thought he was being disrespectful and sent him home for the day. By the time Ricky got home, he was furious and screaming that he wouldn't work at a place that yelled at employees for trying to help. He couldn't understand that his boss wanted him to move on to the next activity because he was perseverating on the need to organize the plants. The use of a Ticket to Perseveration Station (see page 24 for more information on using the Strategic Bombs) here would help Ricky to understand his situation and more easily do what the boss asks.

Situations like these make students look "stubborn," "oppositional," "defiant," and "obsessive-compulsive" – or any combination thereof. You may hear inappropriate language or have to deal with tantrums and meltdowns if the situation is not resolved quickly. The trigger or antecedent behavior may not be negatively oriented, but the outcome will certainly look that way. (There is much more information about this in the Cognitive section of the curriculum.)

The last Strategic Bomb is the **Smart Card**. Individuals with ASD often have impressive amounts of knowledge stored away in their heads that they mistakenly think will be helpful during stressful situations. You will know it is time for a Smart Card when you hear other students or adults saying that the student in question is "arrogant," "condescending," "rude," "ignorant," or using any other word that indicates the person is offended by the student's implied message that they are not smart. While it is one of the more socially irritating and inappropriate coping strategies, it becomes much less offensive to deal with if you remember that the student in question is simply trying to go with what he perceives to be his greatest strength in order to escape a difficult situation. In most cases, it is not meant as a targeted attack even though it looks like one. Let's look at an example.

SMART CARD

In the event that all other conversational strategies fail during stressful interactions, you are allowed to top all other statements by declaring your unequaled giftedness and natural superiority.

Several middle school students were riding the bus on their way back from a field trip to the science center. Morgan, a 13-year-old classmate with ASD, was sitting in a row in front of them. When they began to tease her about wanting to spend so much time looking at a human body exhibit, she got frustrated and began to rock back and forth in her seat. She tried to use her headphones to drown out the students' teasing, but they continued until she finally stood up and yelled, "Well at least I understand what I am looking at. You are too stupid to understand anything but the pictures!" At that point, everyone on the bus knew there was trouble, and the teachers tried to help Morgan calm down.

When they got back to the school, the teacher wrote a note to Morgan's parents about her "explosive episode" and her inability to get along with her peers on the field trip. In reality, Morgan had tried to end a stressful social interaction, but because she couldn't think of anything more appropriate and effective at the time, she ended up getting in trouble and not learning anything from the situation. Chances are that without opportunities to build problem-solving skills, Morgan will continue to inappropriately choose the Smart Card as a coping strategy the next time she is faced with a similar negative social interaction.

Using strategic bombs. The best part about the Strategic Bombs is the many ways that you can use them. Students should view use of Strategic Bombs as a positive way to examine their behavior and learn to identify their strategic mistakes in a safe, forgiving environment. You may want to have students earn points for successful use of Strategic Bombs. Take a look at the ideas below or create your own.

1. Use Strategic Bombs during role-play or group activities by having students discuss their own experiences or scenarios you provide. Examples include a student insisting on finishing the book he is reading before he can go to lunch, getting into an argument with a classmate because of a misunderstanding, or telling a teacher her ideas are stupid. Ask students to talk about how they responded or would respond to the situation and identify whether or not they have accidentally used a Strategic Bomb and what they would do differently next time.

2. Issue a set of Strategic Bombs to each student and tell students that they will receive points or rewards for independently identifying which of the Bombs they used during a challenging situation. If they are successful using this method, reward them for their willingness to try to identify their mistakes. That is progress!

3. After recovering from a meltdown, students can use Strategic Bombs as part of a problem-solving discussion with an adult.

REMEMBER: The discussion or problem solving should NEVER take place until the student has completely recovered and re-entered her daily routine. Students will learn from the situation if they are not trying to manage their emotions at the same time.

Data Collection and Record Keeping

In these times of evidence-based practice and strong emphasis on positive outcomes through effective service delivery, data collection is more important than ever. You are not required to maintain all of the records provided in this book, but you should consider proof of goal achievement and student self-monitoring of goals critical to the credibility of your program – not to mention, the importance of ensuring success for your students.

If you are determined to make the most from the ECLIPSE Model, you will want to maintain the Teacher Checklist, Implementation Record, one form of the Goal Tracking Sheets, and at least some of the student self-monitoring activities and the Behavior Indicator Data Sheet. Used in tandem, these tools will help you to maximize student achievement and progress through the curriculum.

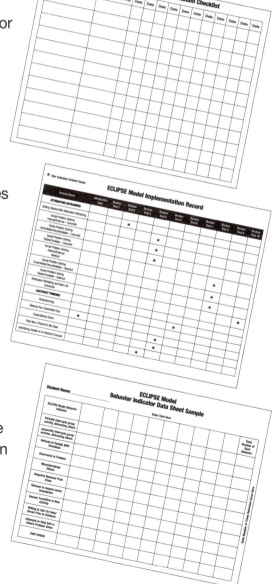

Teacher Implementation Checklist

This provides a timeframe for implementing the major curriculum components. As with the goal-tracking options, you are free to determine how many of these items you are going to include in your use of the ECLIPSE Model.

Implementation Record

This is a quick reference form for recording the dates when each lesson is introduced and reviewed. The stars in each row indicate the Embed Factor (see pages 202-205) for each lesson.

Behavior Indicator Data Sheet

This is a simple tally sheet for recording 10 behaviors that are most likely to be positively influenced by use of the ECLIPSE curriculum. Five consecutive school days or group sessions are usually more than enough to get a snapshot of a student's behavior. Be sure to conduct this data collection once before you implement the lesson so that you can establish a baseline level of behaviors. You are free to determine how often you want to repeat this data collection measure; however, if you are able to use it daily, it won't be long before you can track monthly totals and establish a trend of the progress the students are making.

Behavior Indicator Monthly Summary and Trend Tracker

This sheet provides a log for the accumulated Behavior Indicator Data on a monthly basis. For programs that use more formal data collection methods, this is an excellent summary of behaviors for the team to evaluate any programmatic changes that might be necessary.

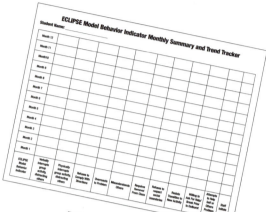

What I Think About My Group! Survey

This survey is for students to complete as a qualitative measure of their progress during implementation of the curriculum. Teachers, group leaders, or parents can gain some insight into students' perceptions of their success in a group environment. If things are going well over time, ideally, there would be evidence of a change to reflect a more positive outlook on the group. Student involvement is an important part of the ECLIPSE Model. Look for the reminder icons at the beginning of each chapter.

Goal Tracking

Each skill area in the ECLIPSE Model includes suggestions for goals that can be used in an IEP or treatment plan. Choose the goal that most closely aligns with the level of skills currently being taught. For example, below are the goals for the Abstract Thinking section of the curriculum. As you will see, the skills named in each goal get progressively more sophisticated. They correspond generally with the lesson plans for each section, which are presented in order of complexity and should generally be completed in that order.

1. Katie will improve her abstract thinking by identifying details that can be grouped to form functional abstract concepts.
2. Katie will learn to "brain storm" abstract ideas in a small-group setting.
3. Katie will improve her social interactions by forming accurate expectations for a given situation.
4. Katie will use abstract thinking to plan life activities through appropriate formation of abstract concepts.

The ECLIPSE Model is designed to give you two choices for tracking goals for individual students. The Abbreviated Universal Tracking Sheet allows you to keep track of up to six goals on the same sheet with spaces to record the targeted behavior or benchmark being measured and the dates when they are achieved. If you prefer to maintain records for each goal separately, use the Universal Goal Tracking Sheet, which allows for space to record the name of the lesson as well. Most of time you will be asked to take data on how often the desired behavior is performed after the lesson has been introduced. To keep the data collection from getting too complicated, you will only be asked to record what the benchmarks are and when they were achieved. Simple tally sheets can be used to record data from individual lessons before the benchmarks are met and the goal is achieved.

When using the ECLIPSE Model, there should be no more than six goals for you and the student to track at any one time. Start with at least one goal from the Self-Regulation and Modulation section. Since successful self-regulation and modulation of behaviors is critical for student progress, you will want to start that immediately and "fill in the blanks," so to speak, with the Attribution Retraining, Cognitive, Social, and Sensory Goals. If you use one goal for each of the five curriculum components, that will leave the sixth goal for you and the student to choose a specific skill that they would like to improve.

Self-monitoring has been shown to reduce disruptive behaviors as well as improve time on task and goal-directed activities such as an art project or packing a backpack to go home for the day. Because of these challenges, the ECLIPSE Model incorporates self-monitoring tools such as My Personal Goal Tracker and My Personal Modulation Tracker.

The Personal Goal Tracker should be used from the beginning of the student's programming, and the Personal Modulation Tracker is introduced at the end of the self-regulation lessons. Remember that student self-monitoring does not alleviate the need for data collection by an adult, but it does instill a sense of personal investment and control in the students and support improved overall performance.

Daily Data Tracker Forms: This is the form that you will use if you are going to track data for each student participating in the lesson. It is a universal form that can be completed for any lesson in the curriculum.

The following table provides guidelines for use of each of the data-collection and record-keeping forms (all forms are included in Chapter 7).

Guidelines for Using Each of the Data-Collection and Record-Keeping Forms

Form	Purpose	Completed By	Frequency
ECLIPSE Model Teacher Implementation Checklist	Provides a comprehensive checklist of curriculum implementation	Teacher or group leader	Prior to implementing the ECLIPSE Model, and then ongoing as instructed
ECLIPSE Model Implementation Record	Provides a record of introduction and review of lessons as well as reaching the Embed Factor for each	Teacher or group leader	Each time a lesson is introduced or reviewed
ECLIPSE Model Behavior Indicator Data Sheet	Provides simple tally sheet for data collection when monitoring behaviors targeted by the curriculum	Teacher, group leader, classroom or personal care aides	Prior to implementation for five consecutive school days or group meetings, and then monthly thereafter
ECLIPSE Model Behavior Indicator Monthly Summary and Trend Tracker	Records monthly summaries of data and identify behavioral trends over time.	Teacher or group leader	Monthly during use of ECLIPSE Model
"What I Think About My Group" Survey	Identifies students' impressions about their progress in the group	Students	Monthly during use of the ECLIPSE Model
ECLIPSE Model Abbreviated Universal Goal Tracker	Maintains a comprehensive record of student goals and benchmarks	Teachers or group leaders	Prior to implementation, and then every time a student participates in activities targeting one of the goals
ECLIPSE Model Universal Goal Tracking Sheet	Provides a detailed accounting of data regarding one specific goal	Teachers or group leaders	Prior to implementation, and then every time a student participates in activities targeting one of the goals
My Personal Goal Tracker	Provides students with a comprehensive record of their goals, benchmarks, and progress for self-monitoring	Students	Prior to implementation, and then every time a student participates in activities targeting one of the goals
Daily Data Tracker	Provides a centralized data collection method for individual student progress	Teachers, group leaders, classroom or personal care aides	During each ECLIPSE lesson that requires data collection, as indicated

References – The ECLIPSE Model: An Overview

American Psychiatric Association. (2000). *Diagnostic and statistical manual of mental disorders* (4th ed., text revision). Washington, DC: Author.

Baron-Cohen, S. (1997). *Mindblindness: An essay on autism and theory of mind.* Cambridge, MA: MIT Press.

Cavell, A. (1990). Social adjustment, social performance, and social skills: A tri-component model of social competence. *Journal of Clinical Student Psychology, 19*, 111-122.

Clark, C., Prior, M., & Kinsella, G. (2002) The relationship between executive function abilities, adaptive behavior and academic achievement in students with externalizing behaviour problems. *Journal of Student Psychology and Psychiatry, 43*, 785-796.

Gioia, G., Isquith, P., Guy, S., & Kenworthy, L. (2000). *Behavior rating inventory of executive functioning.* Lutz, FL: Psychological Assessments.

Kail, R. (2004). Cognitive development includes global and domain-specific processes. *Merrill-Palmer Quarterly, 50*, 445-452.

Kaslow, N. J., Tanenbaum, R. L., & Seligman, M.E.P. (1978). *The KASTAN-R: A student's attributional style questionnaire (KASTAN-R-CASQ).* Unpublished manuscript, University of Pennsylvania, Department of Psychology.

Lee, H. J., & Park, H. R., (2007). An integrated review on the adaptive behavior of individuals with Asperger Syndrome. *Remedial and Special Education, 28*, 132-145.

Lyons, J. M. (1997). *Tunes for knowing and growing* (CD). Marietta, GA: Tunes for Knowing and Growing, Inc. http://www.bitlink.com/jeannelyons/starhome.html.

Martin, J., Mithaug, D., Cox, P., Peterson, L., Van Dycke, J., & Cash, M. (2003). Increasing self-determination: Teaching students to plan, work, evaluate, and adjust. *Exceptional Students, 69*, 431.

Mithaug, D., Agran, M., Martin, J., & Wehmeyer, M. (2003). *Determined learning theory: Construction, verification, and evaluation.* Mahwah, NJ: Lawrence Erlbaum Associates.

Premack, D., & Woodruff, G. (1978). Does the chimpanzee have a 'theory of mind'? *Behavioral and Brain Sciences, 4,* 515-526.

Reynolds, C., & Kamphaus, R. W. (2004). *Behavior assessment scales for students* (2nd ed.). Bloomington, MN: Pearson Assessments.

Schunk, D. H., & Zimmerman, B. J. (Eds.). (1994). *Self-regulation of learning and performance: Issues and educational applications.* Hillsdale, NJ: Lawrence Erlbaum Associates.

Seligman, M.E.P., Peterson, C., Kaslow, N. J., Tannenbaum, R. L., Alloy, L. B., & Abramson, L. Y. (1984). Attributional style and depressive symptoms among students. *Journal of Abnormal Psychology, 93*, 235-238.

Stecker, P., Whinnery, K., & Fuchs, L. (1996). Self-recording during unsupervised academic activity: Effects on time spent out of class. *Exceptionality, 6*, 133-147.

Have you surveyed your students lately?

Chapter 2

ATTRIBUTION RETRAINING AND ASD

Danny is a student with ASD receiving transition services at his high school. Like others in the program, he has a goal to find a part-time job in the community. The local Vocational Rehabilitation specialists suggest that he go on an interview for a job drying cars at a car wash because the work is predictable and there would be a lot of other teens to interact with.

After the interview, everyone agrees that Danny should try the job, but he quits two weeks later. When asked why he quit, Danny explains that his supervisor put him at the front of the carwash line using vacuums that were noisy because that is "where all the rude kids go."

Because Danny assessed the situation and assumed that he was placed with the "rude kids" at one job, he refused to try any new placements for the rest of the school year because he thought that would happen again. Danny's assessment left him feeling he was unsuccessful because he had no way to improve his situation (he had no control over anything), so the only thing left to do was avoid it altogether. He had no motivation to take action and improve his circumstances because his inaccurate assessment made the situation hopeless. This situation could have been avoided if Danny had been able to assess his circumstances more accurately so that he felt he had control over his own outcomes and could improve them when he needed to.

Attribution is our ability to accurately assign cause and effect or motivation to another person's thoughts, words, or deeds, or to the events around us. In other words, it is our ability to connect the dots between the events that happen to us and the reasons why they happen. Some of the situations we attribute are happy or positive; others are negative or just plain bad. Regardless, it is important to assess the circumstances as accurately as possible. It gives us a sense of hope and control over our world, motivates us to take action to improve our circumstances, and, if not done well, causes us to respond inappropriately to social situations or give up on life. It is step 1 of the self-advocacy process. It is that moment in time when we determine what is happening around us – with any luck, it is BEFORE we take any actions.

The cognitive process of attributing or assessing our circumstances has the potential to become a critical instructional element for students with ASD. While extensive research has looked at the attribution patterns of individuals with depression and learning disabilities, as well as successful athletes and business executives, little attention has been shown to the autism community in this regard. What we do know is that (a) there is a significant connection between the development of theory of mind and accurate attribution patterns and (b) many adolescents and adults with ASD also suffer from depression or anxiety.

According to Dr. Simon Baron-Cohen of Cambridge University in England, who pioneered much of the theory of mind association with ASD, as early as 1978, researchers were describing the connection between theory of mind and attribution, with theory of mind being the attribution of mental states to oneself and others (Premack & Woodruff, 1978). Let's look at an example.

If you were at a funeral and saw people crying, you would probably conclude that they are crying because they are sad that someone died. A person with ASD would not necessarily make that connection, even if he is sad himself. Designing an operational curriculum to help individuals with ASD correctly attribute or assess their circumstances was the cornerstone for development of the rest of the ECLIPSE Model.

When an individual does not correctly attribute life events or someone else's thoughts, words, or deeds on a regular basis, it inevitably causes misunderstandings

during social interactions. If left untreated, the person will probably become defensive and overreact in an effort to avoid unpleasant interactions. Long term, this type of attribution pattern will lead to clinical depression as suggested by the reformulated learned helplessness theory. Such a pattern will also become a significant barrier when considering the potential for future behavior changes. That is, right or wrong ... **if you believe that your experiences have been largely unsuccessful or negative, you learn to assume that your future may not be any different**. Without direct instruction or retraining of the attribution pattern, the behaviors will not change.

Say, for instance, that an elementary student with ASD does poorly on a spelling test. When he comes home from school that day and his parents ask how the spelling test went, he says that his teacher made the words difficult so that he wouldn't do well. This is an example of an individual who is unnecessarily assuming that the teacher's motivations toward him were hostile. In reality, it is much more likely that the student didn't study the right words, was feeling bad that day, or any one of a million other reasons.

Most social skills programs start by teaching the individual with ASD self-regulation or anger management techniques. Strategies like asking for a break, counting to 10 before responding, or going to occupational therapy rooms for sensory input are all very helpful, but only if the student has correctly assessed the situation BEFORE all of that. For most of us, this assessment phase happens quickly and accurately enough so that we are not even aware that we are going through the steps in our head. But for individuals with ASD, that is not always the case. One study shows that a third of adolescents with ASD have pessimistic, maladaptive attribution styles.

You may recognize this in one of its most common life examples when a student with ASD is involved in a "mix-up" with another students and says, "He pushed/called me names [the action doesn't matter] because he hates me!" While it is possible that the other student hates the student with ASD, it is also possible that there is a more "neutral" explanation for the action or behavior, such as being in a crowded area or the other student was having a bad day. Because these types of situations cause the most disruption and social isolation for the student, our efforts should focus on correcting the negatively oriented assessments of problem situations.

Parameters for Attribution

The model of attribution theory used in this curriculum was developed in the early 1970s to explain the motivation pattern of students with learning disabilities. At the time, researchers wanted to know why students with learning disabilities appeared to be unmotivated to improve their academic achievement. What they discovered was that the students in question exhibited depressed and hostile attribution patterns like the ones in the examples above. They just plain had no hope for taking control over their circumstances to improve them, so they didn't take any action at all. These researchers found that all human beings have three parameters for their framework of attribution:

1. Locus of causality (internal, external)
2. Stability (stable, unstable)
3. Controllability (controllable, uncontrollable)

Locus of causality examines whether the situation is directly related to something innately characteristic of the person, such as his height, a distaste for certain foods, or special interests or something external. **Stability** is an estimation of the consistency of the circumstances or how often it might change, and **controllability** measures the person's perception of his ability to influence his own outcomes.

Parameters for Attribution

Parameter	Internal	External	Controllable	Uncontrollable	Stable	Unstable
Example idea or event	The fact that you would rather wear sandals than tennis shoes so your feet don't get hot	A rule that says you must be at least 5 ft. tall to ride a roller coaster	How loudly you speak in a library	The weather on the day of your picnic	The rule your mother made that means your room must be clean before you go outside	A thunderstorm knocks down a tree and causes a power outage, leaving you in the dark

After all three parameters have been examined and a general assessment of the circumstances has been made, we should also be able to determine whether we are positively or negatively motivated to action that will improve the circumstances. In other words, the process determines whether or not we have hope. Let's take a look at some examples.

Life Examples

Jamie

Situation: Jamie is in middle school and has a very difficult time transitioning between classes. She carries lots of books, so she does not have to "waste" time trying to return to her locker between classes. On this day, she was bumped by another student and dropped all of her books, which made her late for her next class.

Student Response: Jamie naturally/automatically assumes that the student bumped her on purpose and gets so agitated that she asks permission to see her counselor instead of returning to class. Her assessment of the situation left her feeling that it was **internal** or personal to her and **out of her control** because she would always be the target for abuse by the other student. If she were able to attribute/assess her circumstances more positively, she would see that it was an accident because of the crowded nature of the hallway and likely respond much differently.

Shawn

Situation: Shawn is an 11-year-old who does well in most subjects at school except for math. When his parents question why he has such trouble with math, Shawn explains that there is nothing he can do about it because he has "never been good at it and that will never change."

Student Response: By analyzing Shawn's response, we can see that he has essentially learned to be "helpless" when it comes to math. Based on his experiences, he has decided that his poor math grades are **internal** to him because he has a **stable** or unchangeable lack of natural skills or talents in math. Since he believes that, he also thinks that he couldn't possibly take control to improve his circumstances. Shawn has closed his mind to the possibility of any change, which doesn't leave him with hope, nor does it support positive progress.

Andrea

Situation: When Andrea turned 8, her parents bought her a puppy for her birthday. One of Andrea's challenges is that her sense of hearing is extremely sensitive to high-pitched sounds, so when the puppy barks or whines, she gets very upset. She screams at her mother that the dog is barking on purpose because it knows it hurts her ears.

Student Response: Andrea has negatively attributed that the dog is "out to get" or hurt her. What she does not understand is that puppies, especially, but dogs, in general, bark to protect themselves and others. She is beginning to dislike the dog because she is incorrectly assigning his motive for barking. Andrea has decided that the situation is **external** to her because she believes the dog is the cause of the problem. She has also determined that it is **uncontrollable**, because the dog doesn't like her. In addition, she would likely think it is **stable** because the dog will never like her if it is targeting her. Andrea's attribution probably makes her feel sad or angry and doesn't leave her with much motivation to take action and change her circumstances for the better.

Impact on Development of Other Skills

Achieving a more positive or hopeful attribution pattern is the single most important cognitive skill in the ECLIPSE Model, and it goes hand in hand with self-regulation or modulation of behaviors. That is, students must be able to attribute/assess their circumstances reasonably well in order to self-regulate or modulate their behaviors at the same time. If they can use both together, they will find that they have more successful social interactions and their day is more pleasant.

Attribution is directly connected to theory of mind (see page 93) because, if you are not neurologically able to get inside another person's head or gauge her thoughts and emotions, you will not be able to understand why the other person said or did what she did. Theory of mind is the "What are they thinking/doing/feeling?" whereas attribution is the "Why are they thinking/doing/feeling?" After students have had an opportunity to practice attribution retraining and use it in their daily lives, you should add it to the list of Continuous, Ongoing, Perpetual, and Never-Ending Activities (see page 19).

 Strategic Bomb Alerts! A Perspective Pickle Strategic Bomb would be very appropriate support while teaching attribution Retraining.

Measurable Goals for Learning

Attribution Retraining

Each of the goals below can be used for an IEP or treatment plan based on the student's current programming. The goals are listed in order of skill complexity and correspond to the sequential ordering of the lesson plans for each section. In most cases, there are several lesson plans for satisfying each goal.

Only the goal is included in the ECLIPSE Model. Benchmarks or criteria for measurement, such as "8 out of 10 times weekly for 6 consecutive weeks," must be added by each student's team or primary teacher, as appropriate.

1. Dina will learn to more accurately assess her circumstances using the three parameters of attribution retraining.

2. Kevin will improve his ability to identify situations that are problematic for him through the use of attribution retraining.

3. Zoe will be able to demonstrate the relationship between attribution retraining and self-regulation or modulation of behaviors.

Getting Started

 Objective: To become familiar with the language used during the attribution retraining process.

 Required Materials: Handouts, one complete set for each student: "The First Step to Assessing the Circumstances," "Another Step to Assessing the Circumstances," and "One Last Step to Assessing the Circumstances!," and blank templates by the same titles

 Required Prep Time: 5 minutes

Required Activity Time: 20-30 minutes

 Embed Factor: 2

 Brief Overview:

Step 1: Start by reviewing the concepts below. There are only three very basic questions that you need to answer in order to go through the process. It does not matter which one you start with as long as the process includes all three. Be sure that the students understand the concepts for each question. Use the handouts as a visual to support your discussion, and be sure to point out the "Conclusion" at the bottom of each page.

1. **Is the issue internal or external?**
   Did it happen because of something about you or something else?
2. **Is the issue stable or unstable?**
   Is it something you think will always happen?
3. **Is it controllable or uncontrollable?**
   Is there a way that you can respond that will change your situation for the better?

Step 2: Use the blank templates and brainstorm with students to decide which of the three parameters best describes each of the concepts listed.

Step 3: No data need to be taken for this activity, as it is introductory. You will have an opportunity to test students' understanding of the three concepts in the next lessons.

The First Step to Assessing the Circumstances – Sample

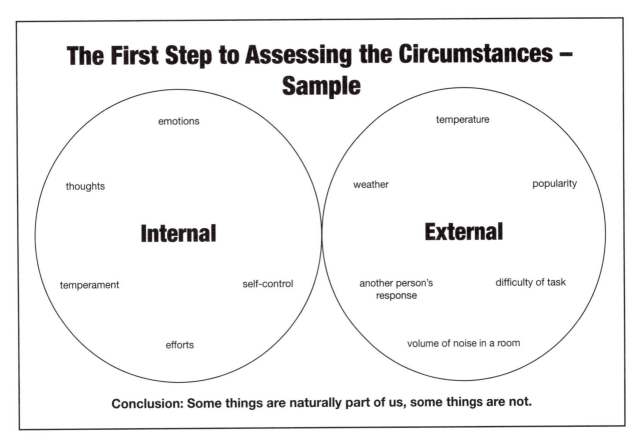

Internal: emotions, thoughts, temperament, self-control, efforts

External: temperature, weather, popularity, another person's response, difficulty of task, volume of noise in a room

Conclusion: Some things are naturally part of us, some things are not.

The First Step to Assessing the Circumstances

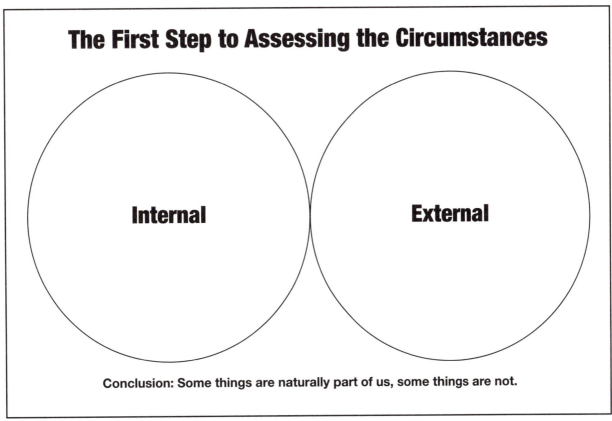

Internal

External

Conclusion: Some things are naturally part of us, some things are not.

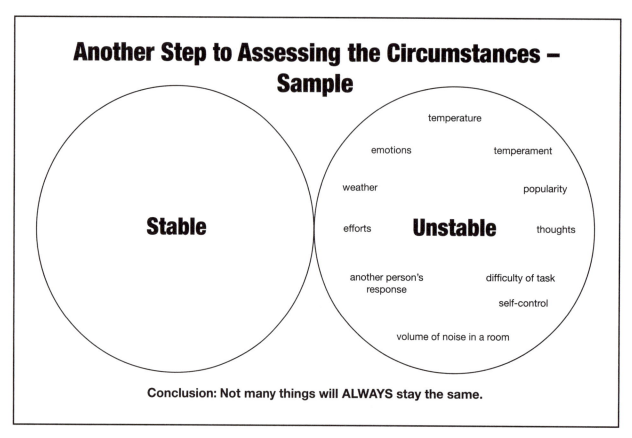

Another Step to Assessing the Circumstances – Sample

Stable

Unstable

temperature

emotions

temperament

weather

popularity

efforts

thoughts

another person's response

difficulty of task

self-control

volume of noise in a room

Conclusion: Not many things will **ALWAYS** stay the same.

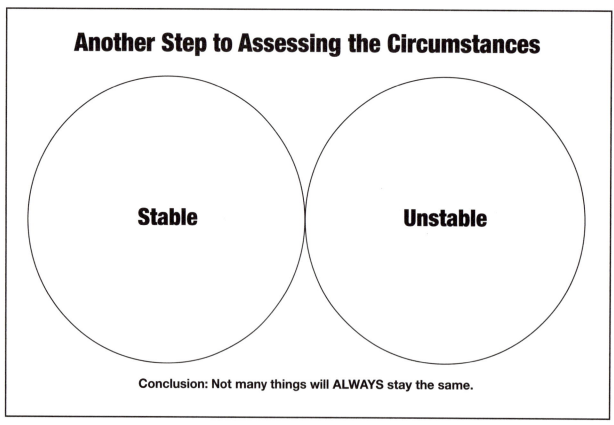

Another Step to Assessing the Circumstances

Stable

Unstable

Conclusion: Not many things will **ALWAYS** stay the same.

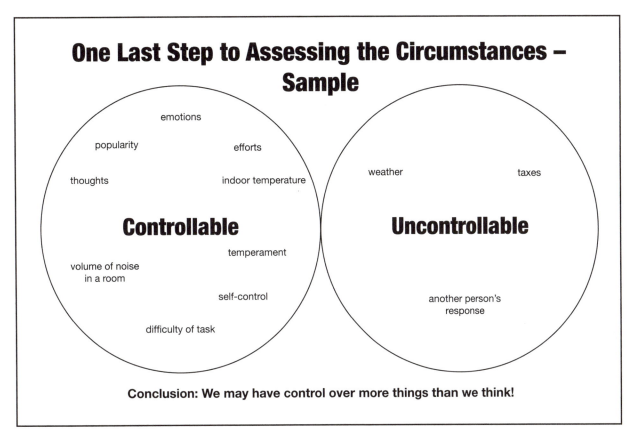

One Last Step to Assessing the Circumstances – Sample

emotions

popularity   efforts

thoughts   indoor temperature

Controllable

temperament

volume of noise
in a room

self-control

difficulty of task

weather   taxes

Uncontrollable

another person's
response

Conclusion: We may have control over more things than we think!

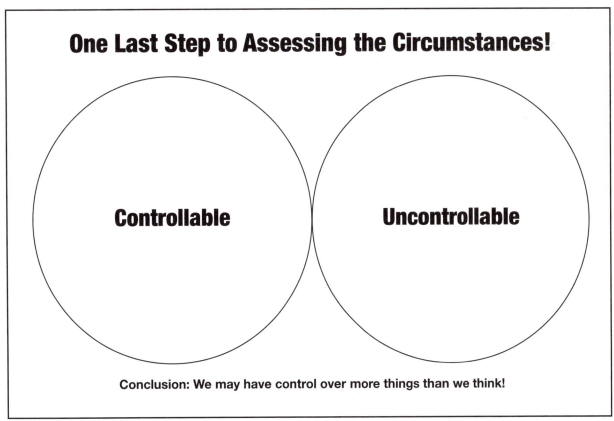

One Last Step to Assessing the Circumstances!

Controllable

Uncontrollable

Conclusion: We may have control over more things than we think!

Attribution Retraining
INTRODUCING THE CONCEPTS OF INTERNAL AND EXTERNAL
(CONCRETE ITEMS ONLY)

 Objective: To apply the three parameters of assessing circumstances to various concrete concepts.

 Required Materials: Chalkboard and chalk or dry-erase board and markers; card stock or other heavy paper; tape; paper and pencils for each student

 Required Prep Time: 10 minutes

Required Activity Time: 30 minutes

 Embed Factor: 4

 Brief Overview: To prepare for the process of learning to assess or attribute situations, we first introduce the three parameters of the process using only concrete concepts. This makes it easier to determine whether or not students struggle with the concepts or the process.

REMEMBER: There may be more than one correct answer for each concept. As long as the context of the student's explanation is reasonable, the answer should be considered acceptable.

The first of these concepts is that of internal vs. external to the self, or individual. For most learners with ASD, abstract concepts or creating concepts from scratch is a great challenge, so gaining expertise through concrete practice is critical to skill performance in the future. Once you have verified that the student has mastered the basic concept in concrete form, you are free to move toward teaching the same concepts with more complicated abstract ideas. Even though there is only one lesson plan, you will repeat it *two more times* so that all three parameters of attribution are covered – so you actually have three lessons in one. It is a good idea to do one at each session with lots of time for practice to ensure learning.

Step 1: Draw two large circles side by side on the chalkboard or white board, labeling one Internal and the other External.

> *For younger student's (ages 5-8 years) or for those with more severe behavioral challenges, such as frequent outbursts that lead to swearing or breaking items, you can use the words Inside and Outside if developmentally appropriate.*

Step 2: Explain to students that they will be labeling things as either Internal/Inside or External/Outside. To do so, they will have to ask and answer the question, "Is this really part of me as a person, or is it about something outside of me?"

Write the following list of words on the board, and as a group discuss in which of the two circles they belong. It is all right to prompt the students or to label one or two of the words yourself to get the conversation started. As each of the words is labeled, be sure to write it inside the appropriate circle.

Eye color	Age
Thoughts	Environment/surroundings
Shoe size	Schedules
Favorite foods	Rules
Weather	Friends

Step 3: Repeat Step 2 by writing each of the words listed below on a piece of card stock with tape on the back. Ask students to take turns choosing a word, labeling it Internal/Inside or External/Outside, attaching the card side in the correct circle, and explaining why they made that choice.

Time (external)	Feelings/emotions (internal)	Money (external)
Traffic (external)	Fears (internal)	Family (external)
Moods (internal)	Sense of smell (internal)	Holidays (external)
Pets (external)		

> *For younger or more severely challenged students, this step may require active prompting or support. Don't be afraid to simplify the choices even further to promote skill acquisition. For example, instead of using the word "thoughts," you might want to say "ideas" or "feelings," and for the words "environment/surroundings," you might want to try a specific area such as a classroom or playground or park. As each of the words is labeled, be sure to place it inside the appropriate circle.*
>
> *Students' answers may vary, but for this parameter, answers are likely to be clear-cut. You may find that a student has a reasonable explanation for choosing the*

opposite parameter of what is correct but that the logic she used to arrive at her answer was faulty. For example, what if a student says that moods are external because they are caused by things or people around her? You would want to re-direct the student by engaging her and the rest of the group in a discussion about external events or circumstances influencing our moods but still being internal to us because they involve our own feelings or emotions. The parameters of stable/ unstable and controllable/uncontrollable are much more open to interpretation, so ask the student for an explanation of her' choices.

Remember that we are trying to move them from a negative attribution to a more neutral or positive attribution that encourages motivation. While you don't want to argue with the student's explanation because that is her perception of the situa-tion, you will find that there are times when you need to engage in further discus-sion to help the student see the alternatives.

For example, if a student says that feelings such as anger are unstable because they "just happen," you might want to a ask question like, "Do you get mad ev-ery time mom changes your plans without telling you?" If the answer is yes, you could suggest that the student "knows that situation always makes her mad so the feeling of anger is stable." This will do two things. It will help the student identify potential problem situations, and it may also help her to be prepared with an ap-propriate response.

Extra Extra! Although there may be some variations, when all of the words have been labeled, the circles should present the visual conclusion that "Some things are part of us, and some things are not."

Step 4: Repeat Steps 1-3 using the parameters of Stable/Unchanging or Unstable/ Changing instead of the Internal/Inside and External/Outside. Use the same list of words as in Steps 2-3. Once each list has been labeled temporarily, pause the group discussion and point out the new conclusion that should become visually obvious, by saying, "Most things are not stable/unchanging."

Step 5: Repeat Steps 1-3 using the parameters of Controllable/Uncontrollable instead of Internal/Inside and External/Outside. Again, use the same list of words as in Steps 2-3. Once each list has been labeled temporarily, pause the group discussion to point out the new conclusion that should become visually obvious, by saying, "We have control over more things than we think."

Next Steps: After each of the parameters has been explored using the words provided, have the students generate and label their own concepts individually and as a group. Write their ideas in each of the circles on the board after they have explained the reasoning behind their choices.

Measuring Success: After Steps 2-5 have been completed, choose five new concrete concepts and write them on the board for the group to see. Here are some examples:

1. Blizzards   2. Information   3. Parades   4. Sickness   5. Vacations

Have the students independently assign the concepts to each of the three parameters (Internal/External, Controllable/Uncontrollable, Stable/Unstable) and write them down. Review students' answers with them individually. Use the Daily Data Tracker to record the results.

Students can be considered to have achieved success when they are able to assign four out of five concepts and provide appropriate explanations for each of their choices. Since you are only testing one parameter at a time and there are five concepts, you should give 1 point for each choice explained appropriately, for a total of 5 possible points for this lesson. Remember that you will be repeating this lesson for each of the parameters of attribution. It is O.K. to test students on the same concepts at the end of each trial as long as they are different from the examples in the lesson.

Attribution Retraining
INTRODUCING THE CONCEPTS OF INTERNAL AND EXTERNAL
(ABSTRACT OR IMPLIED CONCEPTS ONLY)

 Objective: To help students consistently use the three parameters of attribution to accurately assess abstract social situations.

 Required Materials: Chalkboard and chalk or dry-erase board and markers; card stock or other heavy paper; tape; paper and pencils for each student

 Required Prep Time: 10 minutes

Required Activity Time: 30 minutes

 Embed Factor: 8

 Brief Overview: During these exercises, we will follow the same basic steps as we did with the concrete concepts. The first of the three parameters we will explore is Internal/External. This time, the concepts being attributed are abstract, which makes them more challenging for students with ASD.

REMEMBER: There may be more than one correct answer for each concept. As long as the context of the student's explanation is reasonable then the answer should be considered acceptable.

Step 1: Draw the following diagram on the chalk or white board.

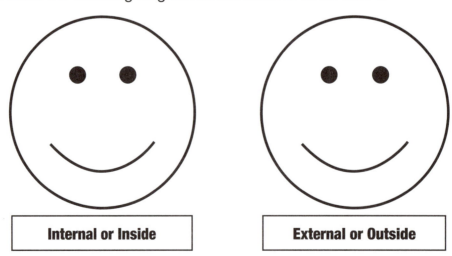

Step 2: Explain to students that they will be labeling things as either Internal/Inside or External/Outside. To do so, they will have to ask and answer the question, "Is this really part of me as a person or is it about something outside of me?"

Write the following list of words on the board, and as a group discuss which circle they belong in. It is O.K. to prompt the students or to label one or two of the words yourself to get the conversation started. As each of the words is labeled, be sure to write it inside the appropriate circle.

Friendship	Trust	Excitement	Happiness
Danger	Truth	Safety	Boredom
Neat	Messy		

Step 3: Repeat Step 2 by writing each of the words listed below on a piece of card stock with tape on the back. Ask students to take turns choosing a word, labeling it Internal/Inside or External/Outside, placing the card in the correct circle, and explaining why they made that choice.

Rage	Silliness/nonsense	Sadness	Fun
Imagination	Peaceful	Scary	Luck
Rude	Polite		

For younger or more severely challenged students, this step may require active prompting or support. Don't be afraid to simplify the choices to promote skill acquisition. As each of the words is labeled, be sure to place it inside the appropriate circle.

Step 4: Repeat Steps 1-3 using the parameters of Stable/Unchanging or Unstable/Changing instead of the Internal/Inside and External/Outside. Use the same list of words as in Steps 2-3. Once each list has been labeled temporarily, pause the group discussion to point out the new conclusion that should become visually obvious, by saying, "Most things are not stable/unchanging."

Step 5: Repeat Steps 1-3 using the parameters of Controllable/Uncontrollable instead of the Internal/Inside and External/Outside. Be sure to use the same list of words as in Steps 2-3. Once each list has been labeled temporarily, pause the group discussion and point out the new conclusion that should become visually obvious by saying, "We have control over more things than we think."

Next Steps: After each of the parameters has been explored using the words provided, have the students generate and label their own concepts individually and as a group. Write their ideas in each of the circles on the board after they have explained the reasoning behind their choices.

Measuring Success: After Steps 2-5 have been completed, choose five new abstract concepts and write them on the board for the group to see. Have the students independently assign the concepts to each of the three parameters (Internal/External, Controllable/Uncontrollable, Stable/Unstable) and write them down. Review students' answers with them individually.

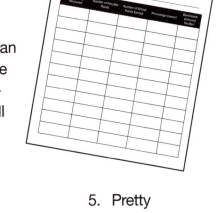

Use the Daily Data Tracker to record the results. Students can be considered to have achieved success when they are able to assign four out of five words and provide appropriate explanations for each of their choices. Remember that you will be repeating this lesson for each of the parameters of attribution. Examples may include:

1. Public	2. Good	3. Bad	4. Nice	5. Pretty
6. Private	7. Mean	8. Ugly	9. Beauty	10. Freedom
11. Kindness	12. Love	13. Heroic	14. Smart	15. Bossy
16. Appropriate	17. Sensitive	18. Famous	19. Power/powerful	20. Selfish
21. Cute	22. Fancy	23. Confusion	24. Rich	25. Poor

Applying Attribution Retraining to Real-Life Scenarios

 Objective: To have students embed the use of the three parameters of attribution into their daily routine.

 Required Materials: List of practice scenarios and handout, "Why Did That Happen to Me?"; chalkboard or white board with chalk or markers

 Required Prep Time: 15 minutes

Required Activity Time: 30-45 minutes, depending on the size of the group

 Embed Factor: 10!
You can never practice this too much! You may want to designate some time before lunch or at the end of the day to have students use real-life examples from their day when going through this activity. Frequency of practice is more important than the amount of time you spend practicing each time. The more often you are able to help students with real-life situations as they pop up during the day, the more thoroughly they will understand how to use attribution to their benefit.

 Brief Overview: At this point in the lessons, practice is the most important influence on successful use of attribution retraining to improve social outcomes. There should be no shortage of ideas for this exercise, since we need to attribute all of our circumstances as we go through the day. Be creative and flexible about the answers you allow, as long as they make sense in the context of the situation being examined.

> *This lesson should also be used whenever you are helping a student process a recent crisis moment but NOT until you are sure he is calm enough to work with you.*

Step 1: Have the full group choose three real-life scenarios from the practice list on page 52.

Step 2: As a group, work through all three steps of the process, so that you all agree on how to assign the parameters of Internal/External, Controllable/Uncontrollable, and Stable/Unstable to each situation.

Step 3: Once you have completed all three steps for a scenario, ask students whether or not they think they can make the situation better based on how they assessed it. Some may say yes and others say no, depending on how positive their assessment or attribution is.

Step 4: After the group has completed three scenarios together, give each student a "Why Did This Happen to Me?" chart and ask them to choose a scenario from the list or to think of one that has happened to them in real life. Have the students complete the first row of the chart, "At First Look." If your students have difficulty with writing, modify the activity by having them dictate their answers to you, an aide, or another student who is more comfortable writing.

Step 5: When all students have completed their own scenarios, ask for volunteers to read their answers. The idea is to get all students to share their thoughts and then have the group discuss each of the situations and explore possible alternatives to the solution that was given. Once the group has discussed a volunteer's answer, ask the student if he would like to change any part of his original answer. If he says yes, have him write his new answers in the second row entitled "On Second Thought." There is no one correct answer, so students are not to make fun of or criticize answers from the other students.

Step 6: Once each day for a week, or at least once during each group session, stop the group at an appropriate moment and have them go through the attribution process to determine why events are happening as they are. For example, there might be an unannounced fire drill in the middle of a class movie, the electricity may go off in the school, or two students may argue about their position in line. There is no limit to the circumstances that you can choose from (see the list on page 52 for ideas).

Extra Extra! This lesson provides several good skill-building opportunities. While you are focusing on the attribution process for real-life scenarios, you are also brainstorming, problem solving, and improving students' abstract thinking. That's a lot in one activity! Your goal is to make this process a natural part of everyday life for everyone in your group, including yourself. Sooner or later, everybody will be so good at it that you won't need visuals, prompting, or spend much time on it at all! The more everyone assesses his or her circumstances using this process, the more the group is likely to see a reduction in disruptive behaviors. Everybody WINS!

Measuring Success: Have students complete a "Why Did this Happen to Me?" chart independently while you watch. Do not offer any answers, since the idea is to assess their attribution retraining performance. If the student is able to complete the chart and explain an answer that is appropriate to the context of the situation, consider the activity a success.

Once the student has successfully used a chart, interrupt her day at some point and ask her to attribute the situation without any charts or visuals to support her. If she is able to do this, the skill has been successfully acquired and demonstrated.

Using the Daily Data Tracker, record data on whether or not the student successfully completed the attribution of a situation using the chart without prompting of ideas or answers by adults.

Why Did This Happen to Me? Sample

	Exactly What Happened?	Was It Internal or External to You?	Was It Stable or Unstable?	Was It Controllable or Uncontrollable?	Assessment or Attribution of the Cause or Motivation	Are You Motivated to Take Action and Improve the Situation?
At First Look	Paul got a much lower grade than normal on a test in his favorite subject at school.	Paul believes that he is no longer as talented at geography as he used to be, so the circumstances are INTERNAL to him.	Paul feels his grade is a reflection of a loss of "talent" on his part, so even though he knows that he has never gotten a "C" grade before, he believes the circumstances are STABLE to him.	Paul is so shocked by the grade that he has absolutely no understanding of why this might have happened to him. He therefore decides that the situation is UNCONTROLLABLE.	Paul believes that there is something wrong with him as a person and that he can no longer achieve at geography.	Not At All! Paul's attribution of the situation is so negative that he is not sure there is any reason to pursue geography as a career.
On Second Thought	Paul got a much lower grade than normal on a test in his favorite subject at school.	Paul's mother points out that he was very sick the day he took the test, so he still believes the circumstances were INTERNAL to him.	Paul decides that since he is hardly ever sick and has never gotten a "C" grade before, the circumstances are UNSTABLE to him.	Paul decides the circumstances are in fact CONTROLLABLE to him because he can choose to take the test when he is feeling better since illness is an acceptable reason for being absent during a test.	Paul understands that his illness likely caused him to do poorly on the test, and even though it is unfortunate, it is an isolated situation.	Sure! Paul is more motivated to avoid the same outcome in the future by choosing to inform the teacher of his illness and arrange for a make-up test.

Real-Life Scenarios for Attribution Retraining – Practice List

1. You spill your glass of milk when you pull a chair in at the dinner table.
2. You take a driver's test and fail because you didn't parallel park close enough to the curb.
3. Your favorite TV show is canceled because of a sporting event.
4. You get a bad grade on a test.
5. You get a good grade on a test.
6. You are forced to change your plans because of bad weather.
7. You forget to bring your homework to school.
8. Your dog or cat accidentally bites you while you are playing together.
9. Your brother steals your favorite skateboard and accidentally breaks it.
10. You get an extra birthday present from your cousins that you did not expect.
11. You get in trouble because you yelled at a teacher.
12. You find your old Gameboy game that you thought you lost under your bed.
13. You want to go to a friend's house, but he tells you that he is not allowed to have anyone over.
14. You cut your leg and have to get stitches at the emergency room.
15. You drink too much soda and throw up.
16. Someone calls you a bad name and pushes you.
17. Someone brushes up against you in the hallway.

References – Attribution and Attribution Retraining

Abramson, L. Y., Seligman, M., & Teasdale, J. D. (1978). Learned helplessness in humans: Critique and reformulation. *Journal of Abnormal Psychology, 87,* 49-74.

Barnhill, G., & Myles, B. S. (2002). Attributional style and depression in adolescents with Asperger Syndrome. *Journal of Positive Behavior Interventions, 3*(3), 175.

Baron Cohen, S. (1997). *Mindblindness: an essay on autism and theory of mind.* Cambridge, MA: MIT Press.

Baumeister, R. F. (1989). *Masochism and the self.* Hillsdale, NJ: Earlbaum.

Blackshaw, A., Kinderman, P., Hare, D., & Hatton, C. (2001). Theory of mind, causal attribution and paranoia in Asperger Syndrome. *Autism, 5,* 147-163.

Bowler, D. M., & Thommen, E. (2000). Attribution of mechanical and social causality to animated displays by children with autism. *Autism, 4,* 147-71.

Carlyon, W. (1997). Attribution retraining: implications for its integration into prescriptive social skills training. *The School Psychology Review, 26*(1), 61-73.

Covington, M. V. (1985). The role of self-processes in applied social psychology. *Journal for the Theory of Social Behaviour, 15,* 355-389.

Klin, A. (2000). Attributing social meaning to ambiguous visual stimuli in higher-functioning autism and Asperger syndrome: the Social Attribution Task. *Journal of Child Psychology and Psychiatry, 41,* 831-846.

Metalsky, G. I., Abramson, L. Y., Seligman, M.E.P., Semmel, A., & Peterson, C. (1982). Attributional styles and life events in the classroom: Vulnerability and invulnerability to depressive mood reactions. *Journal of Personality and Social Psychology, 43,* 612-617.

Meyer, J., Mundy, P., Vaughan Van Hecke, A., & Stella Durocher, J. (2006) Social attribution processes and comorbid psychiatric symptoms in children with Asperger syndrome. *Autism, 10,* 383-402.

Premack, D., & Woodruff, G. (1978). Does the chimpanzee have a 'theory of mind'? *Behavioral and Brain Sciences, 4,* 515-526.

Weiner, B. (1986). *An attribution theory of motivation and emotion.* New York: Springer-Verlag.

Weiner, B., et al. (1971). *Perceiving the causes of success and failure.* New York: General Learning Press.

Chapter 3

Cognitive Skill Development – Abstract Thinking and ASD

Abstract thinking can be defined as the ability to create a "grand plan" or a complete idea in your head. It also includes generating novel thoughts, solutions, alternatives, hypothetical thinking, and flexible interaction with others or the environment. In plain English, **abstract thinking is the ability to take the details of an idea, situation, or item and put them together to create a complete picture in our heads.** Not only do we do this with concrete examples, we are also supposed to be able to do this in hypothetical or imaginary cases.

Individuals with ASD have a heightened awareness of details coupled with deficits in the ability to organize information. In addition, research has demonstrated clear evidence of a universally present and wide-ranging severity of deficits in abstraction abilities in individuals with ASD. These deficits in abstract thinking may be responsible for the narrow range of interests and can negatively affect problem-solving and reasoning skills. In other words, imagine how difficult it would be to generate abstract ideas if you were unable to successfully picture in your mind what exactly is involved in the concept or activity you are thinking about.

55

Life Examples

Scooter

Situation: Mrs. Jones tells the students that they are to write a one-page essay explaining how they would choose whether to go to an amusement park or a museum on their next class field trip.

Student Response: Scooter knows he would like the museum because they have his favorite dinosaur exhibits, so he writes two sentences: "I want to go to the museum. They have dinosaurs." Scooter thinks he has satisfied the assignment and escalates quickly when the teacher says it is not correct.

Issue: What Mrs. Jones really wanted Scooter to do was evaluate the pros and cons of each choice and explain why he made the choice he did. This would require an ability to articulate the concept or abstract idea and then support it with details.

Andrew

Situation: Andrew's mom tells him they are going to his grandma's birthday party on Sunday afternoon.

Student Response: Andrew's only experience with birthday parties is kids' parties. He arrives at Grandma's house only to discover that there are no games, balloons, or pony rides. He has a meltdown, screaming that this party is stupid and that his mother lied about what they would be doing.

Issue: Andrew's only concept or abstract idea of a birthday party is a party for a student/peer, which is very different than a party for an older person. He has very limited idea of what is included under the abstract thought of birthday parties and, therefore, is unable to adjust his thoughts without warning or preparation.

Amy

Situation: Amy, a teen who is transitioning out of school, is asked to participate in her IEP meeting. The rest of the team members ask her to share what she would like to do after she leaves school.

Student Response: Even though Amy loves animals and would do well exploring employment related to animals, she struggles to build the concept of "life after school" in her head, so she quietly says she has no idea what she wants to do. The team responds by suggesting traditional vocational training to sort or shred office materials. Amy is upset to hear the plan, but does not know what to do to change it.

Issue: If Amy were better able to form abstract thoughts in her head, it is possible that she would be able to anticipate what adult life would be like and what type of employment she would be interested in. Because she could not form these ideas efficiently and express her preferences, she was led into a situation that may not be appropriate or to her liking.

Impact on Development of Other Skills

Not being able to form abstract ideas affects a person's ability to transition from one activity to another, problem solve, generate alternative solutions to problems, or plan future life activities. This is a foundation skill that helps to build and improve all of those areas of functioning. Abstract ideas can be as simple as what to have for dinner or as complex as where to live and what job to pursue. Forming abstract ideas is a complex skill that most people perform several times every day. For people with ASD and abstract thinking skill deficits, even the most trivial activity can require great thought, support through direct instruction, and extra time for planning.

 Strategic Bomb Alerts! A Perspective Pickle Strategic Bomb would be very appropriate support while teaching abstract thinking.

Measurable Goals for Learning
Abstract Thinking

Each of the goals below can be used for an IEP or treatment plan based on the student's current programming. The goals are listed in order of skill complexity and correspond to the sequential ordering of the lesson plans for each section. In most cases, there are several lesson plans for satisfying each goal.

Only the goal is included in the ECLIPSE Model. Criteria for measurement, such as "8 out of 10 times weekly for 6 consecutive weeks," must be added by each student's team or primary teacher, as appropriate.

1. Katie will improve her abstract thinking by identifying details that can be grouped to form an accurate abstract concept that demonstrates understanding of the situation.
2. Katie will be able to utilize strategies to "brainstorm" abstract ideas in a small-group setting.
3. Katie will improve her social interactions by forming accurate expectations of the situation.
4. Katie will use abstract thinking to plan life activities through appropriate formation of abstract concepts.

Brainstorming

Objective: To help students form abstract concepts through the brainstorming process.

Required Materials: Chalkboard and chalk or dry-erase board and markers; "Brainstorming" worksheets

Required Prep Time: 10 minutes

Required Activity Time: 30 minutes

Embed Factor: 6

Brief Overview: "Brainstorming" is a term we use for the process of thinking of all the different ideas we can come up with about specific subjects. Sometimes it is to solve a problem, and at other times it is to describe a concept or idea. There are no right or wrong answers in brainstorming, because the goal is to create a long list of possibilities – whether you are in a group or working individually. Some of the abstractions are concepts such as holidays or meals. Others involve problem solving or planning situations, such as choosing between two activities or planning where to get new clothes.

Step 1: Review the following concepts as a group and ask students to generate ideas that you can write on the board. Be sure to explain that everyone's answers should be accepted because the goal is to generate as many answers or ideas as possible.

- **Gym class or lunch in the school cafeteria (concept/thing):** ex. loud noises, bright lights, running around (gym), weird smells (cafeteria)
- **Buying shoes (problem solving):** ex. choosing what type of shoe, determining sizes, choosing store
- **Packing for a trip (problem solving):** ex. knowing where you are going, what clothes to bring, how many days you will be gone

Extra Extra! Start brainstorming concepts that are concrete in nature and work your way to brainstorming for problem solving as students become more proficient. For example, you could start by brainstorming the abstract idea of a zoo, school cafeteria, or science class, and then work your way toward brainstorming to problem solve situations like what to do when you forget your lunch at school, or get sick and miss a day volunteering at the animal shelter. By doing this, students will have a chance to master the process before they are challenged with more abstract ideas of problem solving.

Step 2: Use any one or several of the following worksheets and ask students to complete a brainstorming activity with a partner. Be sure that each partnership gets a different concept. When everyone has completed the activity, have each pair share their answers with the rest oft the group. Ask the group to help generate other ideas to add to each pair's list. Be sure that each pair completes both a concept brainstorm and a problem-solving brainstorm.

Measuring Success: Take data using the Daily Data Tracker for each student by asking them to generate ideas for at least one concept and one problem-solving abstraction. Use concepts or situations that are individualized to each student to encourage successful completion of the task. For example, if the student has a special interest in baseball, ask him to brainstorm ideas for what a baseball stadium is like (concept) and what a player should do if he drops the ball he was supposed to catch (problem solving).

ᵗᵉᵍ

Brainstorming

Idea/Concept: Vacation

List as many ideas as you can think of about a vacation.

_____

_____

_____

_____

_____

_____

_____

_____

_____

_____

_____

_____

_____

Brainstorming

Idea/Concept: Sports game

List as many ideas as you can think of about a sports game.

_____

_____

_____

_____

_____

_____

_____

_____

_____

_____

_____

_____

_____

_____

Brainstorming

Idea/Concept: Restaurants

List as many ideas as you can think of about a restaurant.

_____

_____

_____

_____

_____

_____

_____

_____

_____

_____

_____

_____

_____

Brainstorming

Idea/Concept: Neighborhood

List as many ideas as you can think of about a neighborhood.

_____

_____

_____

_____

_____

_____

_____

_____

_____

_____

_____

_____

_____

_____

Brainstorming

Idea/Concept: Halloween

List as many ideas as you can think of about Halloween.

_____

_____

_____

_____

_____

_____

_____

_____

_____

_____

_____

_____

_____

Brainstorming

Problem Solving: Asking someone for a date
(Use this example wherever age appropriate.)

List as many ideas as you can think of about what to do if you want to ask someone out on a date.

_____

_____

_____

_____

_____

_____

_____

_____

_____

_____

_____

_____

_____

Brainstorming

Problem Solving: Missing the bus to school

List as many ideas as you can think of about what to do if you miss the bus to school.

_____

_____

_____

_____

_____

_____

_____

_____

_____

_____

_____

_____

_____

Brainstorming

Problem Solving: Brother or sister broke favorite Lego creation

List as many ideas as you can think of about what to do if your brother or sister broke your favorite Lego creation.

_____

_____

_____

_____

_____

_____

_____

_____

_____

_____

_____

_____

_____

Brainstorming

Problem Solving: Needing a ride to work
(Use this example for students who are transition age.)

List as many ideas as you can think of about what to do if you need a ride to work.

_____

_____

_____

_____

_____

_____

_____

_____

_____

_____

_____

_____

_____

Brainstorming

Problem Solving: Your computer died!

List as many ideas as you can think of about what to do if your computer dies.

_____

_____

_____

_____

_____

_____

_____

_____

_____

_____

_____

_____

_____

_____

Expectations

One reason for social difficulties may be that we don't have the appropriate expectations for a specific situation. For instance, you might walk into a fast-food restaurant and sit at a table waiting for a waitress to serve you food like at more formal restaurants. If you expected to be served like that, you would probably be upset or disappointed when you discovered that the situation was quite different. Students with ASD are prone to formulating realistic or unrealistic expectations, so it is helpful to practice forming appropriate expectations and what to do if they are not accurate (addressed in the Self-Regulation chapter).

Expectations are the abstract ideas that we form about things we are planning in the future. They are also:

- Something we have learned to anticipate through previous experience,
- Often not spelled out in advance,
- Different for every situation we are faced with, and
- Often a driving force in our emotions when dealing with the real situation.

Life Examples

Dave

Situation: Dave was told that there would be an assembly at school.

Student Response: Because Dave has only been to assemblies that involve music, that is what he expects to find at the upcoming assembly. When he gets there and discovers it is an assembly about the importance of President's Day, he becomes agitated, yells about the assembly being stupid, and runs away down the hall.

Caitlin

Situation: Caitlin's mom says to Caitlin that they need to go to the grocery store. But on the way, she sees the bank and remembers that she needs to make a deposit, so she pulls in without telling Caitlin ahead of time.

Student Response: Caitlin screams in the car about how her mother was lying when she said they were going to the grocery store. She becomes so agitated that her mother chooses to go home instead of to the grocery store.

Impact on Development of Other Skills

Expectations are built on a person's ability to form abstract ideas, and if that ability is challenged in any way, it can cause substantial disruption, impairing the ability to interact with others or in the community. Having appropriate expectations is a key component to being able to self-regulate and self-advocate.

Making Your Expectations Box

 Objective: To have the group work collaboratively to create the Expectations Box that is used in the next lesson during the Expectations game.

 Required Materials: One small to medium-sized cardboard box for each group; arts and crafts materials; markers

 Required Prep Time: 15 minutes

Required Activity Time: 30-45 minutes

 Embed Factor: Immediate!

 Brief Overview: This activity should be completed in small groups of two to three members (no more than four). It is an arts and crafts project that will be used for the Expectations game in the next lesson. It is just a fun, creative activity to prepare for using the box in the game. If the majority of the students are older, they may view this as an immature or "student-ish" activity. You can substitute brown lunch bags or envelopes for the boxes to make the Expectations game more age appropriate.

Step 1: Divide students into groups of no more than four and give each a small to medium-size cardboard box.

Step 2: Have each student decorate or personalize one side of the box with whatever art materials you have available. Also have them sign their name on the side they decorate.

Step 3: Explain that when everyone has decorated one side, they can decorate the top of the box as a group if they wish.

Step 4: Set boxes aside for group session where Expectations game is scheduled.

Expectations Game

 Objective: To determine the different elements that students can expect to find in concepts or problem-solving situations.

 Required Materials: 1 set of "Phase 1 and Phase 2 Expectations Game Pieces" for each group; 1 copy of Concept List for each student; Expectations Boxes (if your students are older, you can use brown lunch bags or envelopes. Be sure to choose the more developmentally appropriate set of game pieces)

 Required Prep Time: 15 minutes

Required Activity Time: 20-30 minutes for each phase

 Embed Factor: 5

 Brief Overview: This game will illustrate the importance of having realistic expectations. Start by identifying the concept and asking students to identify the correct game pieces. Then reverse the process and ask them to look at the game pieces and identify the concepts. In every situation, there are one or two game pieces that won't belong or don't make sense, so the key is to leave out the incorrect pieces.

Phase 1

Step 1: Cut the Phase 1 Expectations game pieces out and place them in the Expectation Boxes or brown paper bags – or any bag that you can't see through. Label each bag with the name of one of the concepts. Put the concept pieces (summer vacation, birthday party, classroom, pet store, holidays) into each of the group boxes.

Step 2: Divide students into two to three small groups. Give each group one bag of pieces to match each of the five concepts.

Step 3: Have students take turns pulling one concept out of the box at a time. Then have the group empty the corresponding bag and identify each of the pieces. Tell them that they are to put only the correct pieces in the box with the concept. There should be one incorrect piece for each of the concepts. When they have completed the pieces for all five concepts, they move to the second phase of the activity.

Measuring Success: Take data using the Daily Data Tracker for each student by counting the number of inappropriate game pieces that they correctly identified. They should be able to tell you which of the pieces does not go with the concept for at least four of the five concepts.

Phase 1 Expectations Game Pieces

Concept: Summer Vacation

Camp	Beaches
Flowers	Popsicles
Grass	Leopards
Friends	No School

Concept: Birthday Party

Ice Cream	Dump Truck
Cake	Prizes
Pinata	Games
Face Painting	Music

Concept: **Classroom**

Desks	Computers
Books	Cars
Chalkboard	Trash Can
Laundry	Pencils

Concept: Pet Store

Hamsters	Fish
Bowls	Pet Food
Cages	Beds
Pet Toys	Candles

Concept: Holidays

Relatives	Presents
Trips	Parties
Microscope	Food
Long Car Ride	Music

Phase 2

Step 1: Place all of the Expectation game phase 2 pieces into the Expectations Box/paper bag. Give each of the groups a list of Phase 2 concepts on page 77.

Step 2: Have each group take turns pulling pieces out of the box. When they have pulled out several game pieces, they should be able to see natural groupings and identify the concepts from the list. When they have identified all of the concepts from the pieces, the activity is complete.

Measuring Success: Take data using the Daily Data Tracker for each student about the number concepts that they correctly identify from game pieces. They should be considered successful if they can identify four out of five concepts correctly.

Phase 2 Expectations Game Pieces

Concept: Visit to Dentist

Drills	Bright Lights
Floss	Fake Teeth
Mouthwash	Mirror
Receptionist	Toothpaste
Doctors	Zebras

Concept: Oceans

Boats	Sharks
Waves	Sand
Sea Weed	Oil Wells
Sting Rays	Trash
Coral	Dogs

Concept: Forests

Ticks	Spiders
Trees	Moss
Campers	Rabbits
Car Wash	Streams
Bears	Birds

Concept: Factory

Assembly Lines	Boxes
Noise	Safety Goggles
Lights	Machines
Time Clocks	Beds
Fork Lifts	Trash Cans

Concept: Arctic Circle

Seals	Reindeer
Icebergs	Cold
Water	Palm Trees
Snow	Walruses
Polar Bears	Whales

Phase 2: Concept List

Draw a line through each concept as your group identifies it.

1. Visit to Dentist
2. Oceans
3. Forests
4. Factory
5. Arctic Circle

77

Paint Me a Picture in My Head

 Objective: To collectively create abstract ideas by building on the sentence created by the person before.

 Required Materials: Floor space big enough for students to lie down without touching each other; art paper; drawing or coloring pencils; markers

 Required Prep Time: 10 minutes

Required Activity Time: 30 minutes

 Embed Factor: 5

 Brief Overview: The idea behind this activity is to have students work in a group to construct a creative story. Have fun by encouraging the students not to be afraid to add silly sentences as long as they can connect each new sentence to the previous one in some way. There will be lots of laughs for everyone; the more nonsense the better!

Step 1: Have everyone in the group lie down on the floor far enough away from each other so that nobody is touching another student.

Step 2: Turn out the lights and ask students to close their eyes.

Step 3: Tell students that they will be creating a silly story by taking turns adding a sentence.

Step 4: Give the first sentence. Say something like "The dog went into the grocery store and bought bones," or "The rabbits built a nest in a bush under my bedroom." The story does NOT have to make sense – it is much more fun if it doesn't. Play for 10-15 minutes, or until each of the students has had several turns to add a sentence or has run out of ideas.

Step 5: For a fun art activity, have students draw pictures of the story they created. When the group has completed their story and art activity, review the story with the group and encourage them to talk about how it was to have to contribute details to someone else's ideas and whether or not they liked working as a group to create the story.

Identifying Details of an Abstract Concept

Objective: To form abstractions through the planning process.

Required Materials: Handouts, "Identifying Details of an Abstract Concept;" chalkboard and chalk or dry-erase board and markers

Required Prep Time: 10 minutes

Required Activity Time: 30 minutes

Embed Factor: 4

Brief Overview: Through the use of the chart on page 80, students will learn to identify and then prioritize (another cognitive skill) the key elements of any given abstract concept. You will use similar charts again in the Self-Regulation section.

Step 1: Start the activity as a full group and have each of the members identify items or elements of the abstract concepts below. Draw three columns on the chalk or white board and label them "Must Have," "Nice to Have," and "Don't Really Need." For each suggestion, ask the student to identify to which column it belongs. If a student struggles with identifying categories, have other students help out.

Step 2: Use each of the three concepts below to go through the process of identifying elements and categorizing them.

1. Making a sandwich
2. Climbing a mountain
3. Painting a house

Step 3: Once the group has completed these three concepts together, break them into small groups and ask them to complete the chart on page 80. After everyone is finished, ask the groups to share one of their concepts. Have other students help to brainstorm ideas for each of the concepts.

Step 4: When the activity is complete, give each student two new concepts, and ask them to complete the chart independently. Examples include going to a movie, completing a homework assignment, or playing a video game.

Measuring Success: Data can be taken using the Daily Data Tracker on whether or not each student can generate elements or items for each of the three categories for each concept. They should have at least one answer for each category for both concepts, giving them a minimum total of six items.

Identifying Details of an Abstract Concept

	"Must Have"	"Nice to Have"	"Don't Really Need"
Planting a garden			
Having a party			
Going camping			
Add your own here			
Add your own here			

References – Abstract Thinking and ASD

Ambery, F., Russell, A., Perry, K., Morris, R., & Murphy, D. (2006). Neuropsychological functioning in adults with Asperger syndrome. *Autism, 10*, 551-564.

Frith, U., & Happé, F. (1994) Autism: Beyond theory of mind. *Cognition, 50*, 115-132.

Meyer, J., & Minshew, N. (2002). An update on neurocognitive profiles in Asperger Syndrome and high-functioning autism. *Focus on Autism and Other Developmental Disabilities*, *17*(3), 152-160.

Minshew, N., Goldstein, G., & Siegel, D. J. (1997). Neurological functioning in autism: Profiles of a complex information processing disorder. *Journal of the International Neuropsychological Society*, *3*, 303-316.

Shift or Mental Flexibility

> **Have you surveyed your students lately?**

Shift, or mental flexibility, as it is sometimes called, is the ability to move from one idea to the next fluidly in your head. It is very important to the development of other skills such as problem solving, transitioning from one activity to another, and engaging in fluent social interactions.

The ability to shift is impaired in the majority of individuals with ASD regardless of their diagnosis, making it a hallmark of an ASD diagnosis. Even though shift is a cognitive skill, it is most recognizable by its behavioral manifestations. For example, it is at least related to or part of the reason why individuals with ASD can appear to be oppositional if they refuse to transition quickly or be socially inappropriate because they cannot stop talking about a specific subject.

In more articulate students with ASD, adults often incorrectly assume that shift is functional due to their seemingly normal communication skills. While there may be a number of reasons why a student is slow to shift, adults often assume that the student is choosing to be stubborn or oppositional. Instead, it is possible that the student is being challenged by the cognitive need to form an abstract idea of the new activity and move to it mentally. Such misunderstanding creates unnecessary tension and anxiety and may lead to negative reinforcement or punishment. What is needed instead is an extra prompt or a few extra seconds for the student to respond.

Another behavioral manifestation that may be due to deficits in shift is the rigid thought process or need for schedules common among individuals with ASD. Sometimes people with ASD become entrenched in their immediate activity or routine to the exclusion of almost everything else. The degree of disruption that this causes varies from person to person but has the potential to interfere significantly in their daily life. The Life Examples will illustrate some of the ways that shift can influence behavior.

There are at least two types of shift – movement from one activity to another (such as thinking of another response) and requiring the use of a schedule to successfully complete a series of activities. Flexibility, on the other hand, might include such activities as changing plans or understanding that there can be more than one way to solve a problem. Both of these skills are critical to fluid social interactions and navigation of daily tasks or routines.

Life Examples

Brian

Situation: Mrs. Jones calls Brian to her desk to review his science project. As she does with all the other students, she asks Brian to think of another solution for the hypothesis he tested.

Student Response: Brian becomes visibly anxious, telling Mrs. Jones that he included the only solution there is and that there is nothing more to talk about. As Mrs. Jones continues to prompt Brian with ideas, he pounds his fist on the project, breaking a piece, and becoming so agitated that he requires a break from his classroom routine to calm himself.

One Possible Solution: If Mrs. Jones had been more aware of Brian's abstract-thinking and shift deficits, she might have been more patient or instructed him on how to complete the process of generating alternative ideas, saving everyone some grief.

Eric

Situation: Eric, 9, has few friends in his neighborhood because he prefers to play only with Legos. He has tried to play with other students in the past, but they don't respond well to his need to control the way they play and his refusal to do anything but play with his Legos. He and his mother have frequent arguments about why he is "so STUBBORN!"

Student Response: Because of his trouble mentally shifting, Eric appears to be controlling, stubborn, and at least a little obnoxious to the other children in the neighborhood. As a result, he is socially isolated and has frequent unpleasant exchanges with his mother.

One Possible Solution: Eric might benefit from direct instruction in how to engage in activities with others or being allowed to experiment or try new things that he might like to do. This would give Eric a chance to expand his base of interests and improve his ability to shift among activities.

Kim

Situation: Kim is 14 and has been bullied at school regularly because of her special interest in American Girl dolls. The other more sophisticated girls at school think she is "babyish" and "weird" and have caused embarrassing moments, when other students laugh at Kim as well. Kim is socially isolated, angry, and depressed and doesn't want to go to school.

Student Response: During the incidents when Kim is being bullied, she often yells at anyone in the area and calls the girls inappropriate names. A couple of times, she also tried to hit the girls and pushed a teacher who tried to stop her. She has reported being angry because she believes she is the only one who gets in trouble. On these days, Kim comes home and goes straight to her room. When her mom asks her to explain, she cries and says she "hates everybody at school," but she doesn't understand why she "can't keep playing" with her dolls.

One Possible Solution: A counselor or teacher along with Kim's parents could help her to develop more "age-appropriate" interests that might keep her from being bullied and help her to develop peer relationships. Perhaps she could be directed toward fashion, clothing design, music, or some other interest that would allow her to talk with her classmates socially.

Impact on Development of Other Skills

It is important to remember that students with ASD need extra time to process all of the information necessary to respond to our requests or the world around them. Because deficits in shifting are compounded by deficits in abstract thinking to form concepts, the cumulative effects of these skill deficits can easily impede students' ability to progress through their day as well as their ability to master new skills.

The introduction of hidden curriculum items or rules (see the section on Hidden Curriculum, page 112) may be very helpful to improving shift. For example, in Kim's situation, it may have been effective to explain to Kim that not many girls her age still like American Girl dolls, so it would be better to find friends who do or to keep it as a private interest or hobby. Introducing the element of hidden curriculum or unwritten social expectations might allow Kim to improve her understanding of how to balance or shift between her own interests and the expectations or needs of others. It is an important global function that deserves time and effort to develop successfully.

 Strategic Bomb Alerts! A Ticket to Perseveration Station Strategic Bomb would be very appropriate support while teaching shift/flexibility.

Measurable Goals for Learning
Shift or Mental Flexibility

Each of the goals below can be used for an IEP or treatment plan based on the student's current programming. The goals are listed in order of skill complexity and correspond to the sequential ordering of the lesson plans for each section. In most cases, there are several lesson plans for satisfying each goal.

Only the goal is included in the ECLIPSE Model. Criteria for measurement, such as "8 out of 10 times weekly for 6 consecutive weeks," must be added by each student's team or primary teacher, as appropriate.

1. Gina will improve her ability to shift from one abstract thought to another.
2. Gina will identify transitions and changes that occur naturally in her environment.
3. Gina will demonstrate improvement in her ability to transition from one activity to the next.
4. Gina will identify at least three ways in which effective shift or transitioning affects successful social interactions.

The Beginnings of Change

 Objective: To build tolerance for activities that change.

 Required Materials: Interesting activities or books – be sure to have enough materials to create one station for each student

 Required Prep Time: 15 minutes

Required Activity Time: 30-45 minutes

 Embed Factor: 3

 Brief Overview: Being able to successfully shift from one idea to another helps build a tolerance for change. It is human nature to resist change, but individuals with ASD are challenged by skill deficits that make change, shifting, or mental flexibility even tougher. Use your creativity to encourage students to explore change safely through pictures, discussion, or experimentation in the classroom and in the community.

Step 1: Gather up books, magazines, posters, music, or any fun or unusual science activities you can find and spread them out in stations on tables or desks in the room. For example, at one station students may use headphones to listen to music from other cultures, at another they may make homemade play dough or slime, and at yet another they may try a new puzzle.

Step 2: Allow students to freely explore the items, the only rules being that they must try each of the activities and wait, when necessary, to get a turn at an activity. The objective is to encourage students in an informal way to test different activities with no pressure to achieve specific goals. However, they must try at least one thing that they have never done before. Allow 15-20 minutes to complete this step.

Step 3: After everyone has had time to experiment, bring the group together for a conversation about the new things they tried and the way it felt to do few different activities in a short time. Allow everyone to express their opinions freely and without judgment. You are building trust between students and yourself as well as encouraging students to develop trust in their environment and change.

Extra Extra! If you find that a student is anxious about trying new activities or shifting from one activity to the next, you may want to reduce the number of activities that they are required to complete, give them a chance to practice prior to participating with the group, or have another student act as a peer mentor to help them complete the stations.

Step 4: No data are taken for this introductory activity.

The Sounds of Change

 Objective: To increase tolerance for change or transition through the use of music.

 Required Materials: Different kinds of music and a CD player or radio; paper and pencil for each student

 Required Prep Time: 15 minutes

Required Activity Time: 30-45 minutes

 Embed Factor: 2

 Brief Overview: According to the American Music Therapy Association (www.musictherapy.org), music therapy can be used to promote wellness, manage stress, alleviate pain, express feelings, enhance memory, improve communication, and promote physical rehabilitation. Even though the ECLIPSE Model doesn't employ formal music therapy interventions, the students in your group can still benefit from using music to identify changes in their environment. In the same way that adults play music while doing housework or mowing the yard to make the task more pleasant, some students will enjoy activities and learn more by adding music to the mix.

Step 1: Gather several different types of music (if you have a "mix" tape or CD that would work well).

Step2: Make sure students have a small piece of paper and a writing instrument.

Step 3: Turn the lights out and have students close their eyes so that the environment is relaxing and conducive to focusing on sounds instead of visual stimuli.

Step 4: Play different types of music in a row for 2-3 minutes. Have students count the number of changes or transitions in the music that they heard and record them.

Step 5: Vary the length of time that you play music as well as the number of times you change the music. After 15-20 minutes, have the group discuss the types of music they heard, as well as the number of changes they noticed. Be sure that each student explains whether she preferred fewer or slower changes to quick or numerous changes.

Step 6: No data are taken for this activity. It is meant to be a way to make students comfortable with change in a fun and nonthreatening way through the use of music.

No Perseveration Station, Please!

Objective: To demonstrate mental shifting during everyday activities.

Required Materials: A variety of small activities that are quickly completed such as word searches, short articles to read, pictures to color, or short board or card games. Try to include activities that appeal to the students' special interests. You will also need pens or pencils and paper for each student and a short checklist that names each activity that is available.

Required Prep Time: 20 minutes

Required Activity Time: 45 minutes

Embed Factor: 4

Brief Overview: This lesson is designed to provide students with an opportunity to learn the skill of shifting between activities without fear of being judged for making mistakes. Like all of us, students with ASD avoid situations that leave them vulnerable to making mistakes. However, students with ASD are often confused about the task demands at hand and become anxious, making any other decision making much more difficult.

Step 1: Set up stations in the room with the same number of activities as the number of students. Activities should be able to be completed within 2-3 minutes; all of them should be different.

Step 2: Give each student the checklist of activities and a pen to carry and instruct them, as they complete each station, to mark it off on the paper. Be sure to tell students that they may not be able to complete all the activities within the allotted time, and that it is O.K.

Step 3: Explain to students that they are to work their way through the activities and that you will signal when it is time to move on to the next station. They are only to check off the station number on their list if they have completed the activity.

Step 4: Start by giving them 3 minutes at each station. This should be plenty of time to complete one activity while not causing too much anxiety.

Step 5: Repeat Step 4, but this time allow only 2 or 2.5 minutes for each activity, depending on how well the group was able to complete Step 4. If a student has partially completed an activity during a previous round of stations, allow him to set it aside and continue to complete it during the next round if he would like.

Step 6: After the second trial, have the group discuss how they felt as they were working with more time at each station. Were they more anxious with less time? Ask them how they like having to go through several stations at once. Some students may be comfortable and enjoy the pace while others are agitated by the faster pace or the number of activity stations.

Step 7: Take data using the Daily Data Tracker on the number of stations the students successfully complete. You will have two time trials essentially, so you can record data for the longer time and number of stations completed versus the shorter time and number of stations completed. Ideally, this will provide some insight into how well each student does when pressured to complete multiple tasks in a row. For example, you may find that some students are more proficient at working quickly whereas others may need additional time to process the information, complete the activity, and move on to the next.

NOTE: You can repeat this activity as many times as you wish as long as you can find activities that the students can complete quickly. As you make more demands for rapid shifting, students may become anxious or their behavior may escalate. A little frustration is not a bad thing, but be careful not to push students too far beyond their tolerance for change, or you may be faced with a meltdown!

References – Shift and Mental Flexibility

American Music Therapy Association, Inc. *What is music therapy?* Retrieved on January 15, 2009, from www.musictherapy.org.

American Psychiatric Association. (2000). *Diagnostic and statistical manual of mental disorders* (4th ed., text revision). Washington, DC: Author.

Ambery, F., Russell, A., Perry, K., Morris, R., & Murphy, D. (2006). Neuropsychological functioning in adults with Asperger syndrome. *Autism, 10,* 551-564.

Lyons, J. M. (1997). *Tunes for knowing and growing* (CD). Marietta, GA: Tunes for Knowing and Growing, Inc. http://www.bitlink.com/jeannelyons/starhome.html.

Ozonoff, S., Rogers, S., & Pennington, B. (1991). Executive function deficits in high-functioning autistic individuals: Relationship to theory of mind. *Journal of Student Psychology and Psychiatry, 32,* 1081-1105.

Prior, M., & Hoffman, W. (1990). Brief report: Neuropsychological testing of autistic students through an exploration with frontal lobe tests. *Journal of Autism & Developmental Disorders, 20,* 581-590.

Rumsey, J. M. (1985). Conceptual problem-solving in highly verbal, nonretarded autistic men. *Journal of Autism & Developmental Disorders, 15,* 23-36.

Shu, B. C., Lung, F. W., Tien, A. Y., & Chen, B. C. (2001). Executive function deficits in non-retarded autistic students. *Autism, 5*(2), 165-74.

Have you surveyed your students lately?

Chapter 4

Social Skills Development – Theory of Mind and ASD

Over the years, theory of mind as it relates to ASD has evolved to become the foundation of the social theory of autism. In plain English, **theory of mind refers to our ability to read others' minds.** That is, it is the ability to assess and project the thoughts, feelings, or "mental" actions that are going on inside another person's head. Talk about a social skill!

Imagine for half a second how difficult it would be to interact socially if you had no reasonable estimation of what the other person was thinking. Say, for instance, you see two people standing at a street corner talking in an animated fashion. Unless you were able to interpret the content of their conversation and add it to the physical clues of their actions and environment, you could explain their behavior in any of the following ways.

Situation: Two people are standing at a street corner talking in an animated fashion.

Possible Interpretations of the Situation:
1. Two people are arguing at the street corner about directions.
2. One person is being attacked at the street corner and trying to defend himself.
3. Two people at the street corner are imitating flapping birds to be silly.
4. One of the two persons at the corner is deaf and is communicating through sign language.
5. The two people at the corner are professional musicians and are practicing conducting an orchestra.

Ask a person with ASD to describe what she witnessed in this case. She will probably give you a meticulous, detailed description of the visible physical conditions of the environment. If you ask that same individual why the two people were behaving the way they were, you may get any one of the five answers above, underlining her difficulty in putting herself in somebody else's shoes.

Theory of mind involves identifying mental states in another person, and for individuals with ASD this skill is significantly challenged. Mental states can include wishing, planning, thinking, guessing, wanting, and any other behavior that can be accomplished exclusively inside our heads. Not every behavior we carry out is visible to the rest of the world. For those with ASD, recognizing the idea that other people carry out behaviors in their heads is like a mystery to be solved. Individuals with ASD are not prone to assessing or projecting others' covert actions, thoughts, or emotions, so they are left to create explanations and solve these mysteries on their own. Sometimes this can lead to very inaccurate ideas and responses on the part of the student with ASD. (See the Life Examples below.)

Researchers are pursuing several neurological explanations for this skill deficit, including eye gaze pattern and early development of skills called joint attention, or the shared attention mechanism. Individuals with ASD do not look at faces in the same way as the rest of us. As a result, they are not able to gauge the affect or mood of others.

The purpose of joint attention or the shared attention mechanism is to give us an internal "drive" to establish a shared interest or common ground with another person. So, due to impairment in this area, it is not unreasonable to say that an individual with ASD has little, if any, neurological awareness that other people conduct the same activities in their heads as they do. Further, because these skills emerge early in life, other more sophisticated social and communicative skills that normally follow do not emerge, at least not fully.

Theory of mind is such a natural part of our world that it is difficult to imagine life without any functional capacity in this realm. We must be careful not to confuse theory of mind with attribution (see Chapter 2 on Attribution Retraining). Theory of mind answers the question, "**What** are they doing in their heads?" whereas attribution answers the question, "**Why** are they doing that?" Together, use of these two skills can help to prevent frequent social misunderstandings and overreactions. From the real-life examples below, you will see how confounding it can be for an individual with ASD when theory of mind is compromised.

Life Examples

Ethan

Situation: Ethan, 15 years old, has very sensitive hearing in addition to his ASD. His mother has a pet parrot that talks and generally is quite noisy, so Ethan doesn't tolerate the bird well. Yesterday Ethan knocked over the parrot's cage, and when his mother asked why he did it, he answered, "the bird made too much noise because it knew it would hurt my ears."

Student Response: Ethan is personifying the bird and assuming that it wants to hurt his ears in a purposeful way. He has no recognition of the fact that talking and other noises are typical behaviors of a parrot. Because he doesn't know, he assumes an aggressive stance on the bird's part, contributing to his overreaction.

Lexi

Situation: Lexi is a 12-year-old who attends middle school. While she was walking down the hallway at school, she saw a classmate coming toward her but then suddenly turning around and walking the other way. By the time Lexi got to class, she was crying. When the teacher asked why she was upset, Lexi explained that she thought the boy had turned around on purpose because he saw her and wanted to avoid her.

Student Response: Lexi got upset because she incorrectly assessed what the boy was thinking. Trying to help her, the teacher asked the boy what happened. He explained that he realized he had forgotten a book in his locker and had turned around and run back so he wouldn't be late for class. A perfectly benign situation turned negative because of a lack of theory of mind.

Brandon

Situation: Brandon, an 8-year-old, was involved in an altercation with one of the neighborhood students. His mother asked him how he thought the other student must feel after being treated so poorly. Brandon answered that he had "no idea and didn't care" what the other student felt, making him sound cold and callous. Brandon's mother was so upset by this answer that she didn't allow Brandon to go outside to play for a whole week.

Student Response: When Brandon stated that he had no idea what the other student was thinking, he was probably telling the truth. Even though it sounded as though he was uncaring, and deserving of severe consequences, he may genuinely not have any idea of what goes on inside another person's head.

Impact on Development of Other Skills

From the information above, it should be clear that theory of mind directly affects attribution skills and that deficits in this area negatively influence social interactions. Problem solving, social competence, and school or community program placements can all be in jeopardy when theory of mind fails us. Take for example the student with ASD who is frequently in trouble at school because he inaccurately believes the girls who are friendly or helpful to him are his "girlfriends." He doesn't understand that they only mean to be friendly and are not attracted to him romantically so it often leads to awkward or angry conversations with the girls and calls home to his parents by the principal. The friends of these girls will isolate him socially, and other girls will be afraid to show him any kindness at all. Further, teachers, the principal and his parents are all likely to think he is not behaving appropriately. As a result of all this, he is likely to become depressed at his lack of friends.

All of this could have been avoided if this student had been able to understand the true intentions of his female classmates who were just being nice. What was a fairly simple situation has now taken perhaps weeks or months to resolve with very sad outcomes. Theory of mind should be considered a vital skill that significantly affects the outcome of social interactions all day, every day.

 Strategic Bomb Alerts! A Perspective Pickle Strategic Bomb would be very appropriate support while teaching theory of mind.

Measurable Goals for Learning
Theory of Mind

Each of the goals below can be used for an IEP or treatment plan based on the student's current programming. The goals are listed in order of skill complexity and correspond to the sequential ordering of the lesson plans for each section. In most cases, there are several lesson plans for satisfying each goal.

Only the goal is included in the ECLIPSE Model. Criteria for measurement, such as "8 out of 10 times weekly for 6 consecutive weeks," must be added by each student's team or primary educator, as appropriate.

1. John will identify at least 10 different mental states or actions that can be carried out in a person's head.
2. John will demonstrate at least five strategies for determining the mental states of others.
3. John will identify at least five situations that he has experienced personally that are negatively affected by theory of mind deficits.

What Are They Thinking?

 Objective: To identify as many mental states as possible.

 Required Materials: Handout, "What Are They Thinking?" head silhouette for each student

 Required Prep Time: 10 minutes

Required Activity Time: 30 minutes

 Embed Factor: 3

 Brief Overview: Individuals with ASD can often identify or at least explain what is going on in their own heads; however, theory of mind deficits keep them from doing the same for others. Awareness of activities that can be accomplished in our own heads is the first step toward recognizing the same actions in others.

"What Are They Thinking?" Head Silhouette

Step 1: Give each student a copy of the "What Are They Thinking?" head silhouette.

Step 2: As a group, brainstorm two or three examples of different mental states or actions that people can perform in their heads. Examples include hope, wish, and dream.

Step 3: Allow students to work on their own for 10-15 minutes and ask them to list as many mental states as they can inside the silhouette – at least 10, if possible.

Step 4: After everyone has completed his or her list, have them share some of their answers. Be sure that everyone has an opportunity to contribute and explain any answers that seem unusual in any way.

Step 5: Take data using the Daily Data Tracker for this activity by counting the number of mental states or actions that each student has listed.

Extra Extra! Most of the words designating mental states are verbs or action words. Even though we can't see or touch the things that are going on in our own or anyone else's head, we can still carry out actions in our heads.

Step 3: Choose at least five different pictures and repeat Step 2 with the group so that they are comfortable with the process of gauging social expectations based on dress.

Step 4: Give the students magazines that they can cut apart. Ask them to find a picture of someone that they can describe to the rest of the group.

Step 5: As each student completes his or her turn, ask the rest of the group if they can think of any place where the person depicted should NOT go dressed the way he or she is. Students should be able to describe the obvious characteristics of the person in the picture, and should also include a discussion of the person's clothing and where he or she might be going dressed that way. For instance, if someone is dressed in a tuxedo or a ball gown, he or she is obviously not going swimming or camping.

Step 6: No data are taken for this introductory activity. By using the concrete nature of clothing or types of dress, we can help students understand that many of the things we choose to do, or are required to do, are based on the unwritten social rules around us.

Hidden Curriculum in a Social Environment

Objective: To practice functional strategies for determining the hidden curriculum rules of social situations.

Required Materials: Clipboard or pad of paper and pens for each student; handout, "Diagnosing Hidden Curriculum," for each

Required Prep Time: 10 minutes

Required Activity Time: 30 minutes

Embed Factor: 6

Brief Overview: This activity is designed to use a medical model to "diagnose" the hidden curriculum of a social environment. When we focus on concretely defined concepts such as dress or jobs, it is much easier to make at least a good guess about the social expectations of given situation. More abstract hidden curriculum items, like expected behaviors, are much more difficult to predict, especially for individuals with ASD. Most individuals with ASD are quite good at observing the physical details of an environment, but they are not good at using those details to formulate accurate social or behavioral norms.

Step 1: Give each student a clipboard or a pad with paper and a pen. Explain that they are now doctors or forensic scientists and that it is their job to identify the rules of the hidden curriculum. Examples might be the hidden curriculum of how to behave at a place of worship, order lunch at a fast-food restaurant, or what to do when somebody gives you a present that you already have.

Step 2: Brainstorm strategies for identifying the hidden curriculum in various situations. Examples include asking questions like "How should I behave?" or "What are the rules?" Other ideas might include looking for clues about how other people in the same situation are behaving, how they are dressed, or what they say. One example might be that if you need to ask your teacher a question in class, it is more acceptable to wait until she is not talking to anyone and raise your hand than it is to just call out your question. In order to figure this out, you might watch what other students are doing, or you may take notice of what the teacher does when someone calls out before you do.

Step 3: Give each student a "Diagnosing Hidden Curriculum" sheet and divide them into pairs. If you are in a school and the pairs can move around to a gym or cafeteria, for example, that is great. If not, assign one social situation to each group like being at the library, in the neighborhood, or at the doctor's office.

Step 4: Give each pair 10-15 minutes to diagnose the situation. You may need to help students brainstorm or give them tips on how to find clues.

Step 5: When everyone is finished diagnosing, have each pair present their findings to the rest of the group. Ask them what they thought was easy about the "case" and what was challenging. Encourage the rest of the group to fill in any clues or ideas that may be lacking.

Step 6: Take data using the Daily Data Tracker by asking students to list strategies that they used to determine the hidden curriculum. Their success will depend on how extensively Step 2 is developed, so be sure to give that step plenty of time and energy. Each student should be able to identify at least three strategies for revealing the hidden curriculum, such as asking questions, reading signs, watching what others are doing, etc.

Diagnosing the Hidden Curriculum

Case (situation):

Symptoms or characteristics (what is happening?):

Strategies for diagnosing the situation (how to reveal theory of mind):

What is the recommended treatment (how should I behave)?

Becoming a Hidden Curriculum Detective

Objective: To use a collaborative approach to identifying hidden curriculum rules for specific situations.

Required Materials: One "Hidden Curriculum Activity" sheet for each student

Required Prep Time: 10 minutes

Required Activity Time: 30 minutes

Embed Factor: 3

Brief Overview: This activity continues to build students' skills at revealing unwritten social expectations for any situation. Similar to the Hidden Curriculum in a Social Environment activity, each student is responsible for detecting the hidden curriculum of an assigned situation, but this activity is meant to be completed individually.

Step 1: Randomly distribute one of the three versions of the "Hidden Curriculum Activity" sheet to student. Give them a maximum of 15 minutes to complete their "case," and only help if students specifically ask you.

Step 2: Direct each student to list as many ideas as possible for his or her situation. Each page includes at least two examples to get them started. The activity will challenge students to use their abstract thinking to identify as many details as possible that affect how you should behave in the given situation.

Step 3: Ask each student to list at least five items of their own.

Step 4: When everyone has finished, ask them to share their ideas with the rest of the group. Encourage other students to add ideas to the list if possible. Ask them to point out how the hidden curriculum differs by age, gender, situation, or even culture.

Step 5: Take data using the Daily Data Tracker by counting the number of reasonably identified items listed.

The ECLIPSE Model

Hidden Curriculum Activity

Having Friends Over to Spend the Night

1. Your friends arrange to have enough blankets and pillows so everyone has his or her own, or ask to bring their own.

2. Usually, boys and girls don't spend the night at the same house unless they are family members.

3.

4.

5.

6.

7.

8.

9.

10.

11.

12.

13.

14.

15.

Hidden Curriculum Activity

Going to a Movie With Friends

1. Once the lights go down in the theater, it is not polite to talk during the movie.

2. Try to leave at least one seat between you and any person you don't know unless you don't have any choice (that is, there are no empty seats).

3.

4.

5.

6.

7.

8.

9.

10.

11.

12.

13.

14.

15.

Hidden Curriculum Activity

Eating at a Restaurant

1. Try to speak just loud enough for the people at your table to hear you and not loud enough for people at other tables to hear you.

2. If you taste something bad in your food, it is polite to quietly spit it into your napkin without making any comments about what you are doing.

3.

4.

5.

6.

7.

8.

9.

10.

11.

12.

13.

14.

15.

Keeping a Hidden Curriculum Diary

 Objective: To establish generalization of hidden curriculum skills at home or in the community.

 Required Materials: Handouts, "My Hidden Curriculum Diary Sample" and "My Hidden Curriculum Diary," for each student

 Required Prep Time: 10 minutes

Required Activity Time: 30 minutes at home

 Embed Factor: 4

 Brief Overview: This activity requires a more long-term observation of social environments. Using clear concepts, each student will watch for possible hidden curriculum items related to age, place, gender, people you are with, school, and work.

Step 1: Give each student the example "My Hidden Curriculum Diary." Review it as a group, discussing each example and brainstorming ideas for other items that could be listed.

Step 2: Send home the example page and the blank "My Hidden Curriculum Diary" page and tell students to look at and write down at least two ideas for each category before the next session. Inform parents or caregivers that the assignment is to be completed for the next session. The idea is to build awareness of hidden curriculum in environments outside of the group.

Step 3: At the next session, ask students what they discovered at home or in the community. Be prepared that some students may have forgotten their assignment. If this happens, offer them another page to complete in the group.

Step 4: Take data using the Daily Data Tracker for each student on the number of items completed in the diary page. There are six categories with two samples each, so there should be at least 12 answers. You can consider the activity successful if the student has included at least 9 ideas as long as all 6 categories have at least 1 answer.

My Hidden Curriculum Diary – Sample

Age	By the time I am age 12, people expect that I can cut my own food when I am eating. People might think you are "weird" if you play with little toys if you are a teenager.
Place	It is O.K. to be loud at a football game or when outside with friends, but it is not O.K. to be loud when at a movie or watching a play. It is appropriate to take off my hat at the dinner table.
Male/Female	Men don't normally call each other "boyfriends" whereas women can call each other "girlfriends" without social stigma. Men don't wear make-up, but many women do.
People You Are With at Home or in the Community	My friends may think it is funny when I burp out loud, but my parents or teachers will probably not think so. At a place of worship, it is not appropriate to rock and roll to the music while others are singing religious music.
School	It is considered appropriate to be clean when I go to school. It is polite not to speak out in class without the teacher calling on me first.
Work	I should not make noises that disturb my coworkers. I should not wear too much perfume or cologne at work, because it may make other people uncomfortable.

Hidden Curriculum and Self-Regulation

 Objective: To recognize the functional connection between an understanding of the hidden curriculum requirements for any given situation and the natural consequences that may occur when they are not followed.

 Required Materials: Handouts, "What Would Happen If I Didn't Know That …," and a completed Modulation Chart for each student

 Required Prep Time: 10 minutes

Required Activity Time: 30 minutes

 Embed Factor: 6

 Brief Overview: This activity might more appropriately be called "the laws of natural consequences." Through this activity, students should see that logical and natural consequences occur when we violate the hidden curriculum. Whether we like it or not, our actions have consequences, so why not make the best of it by trying to get it "right" the first time?

Step 1: Give each student a copy of "What Would Happen If I Didn't Know That …" handouts.

Step 2: As a group, brainstorm answers to the three situations and write them in the consequences column.

Step 3: After the consequences column has been completed, ask each student to take a few minutes to complete the self-regulation column on their own. They should be thinking about answers that describe their self-regulation AFTER the consequence has happened. It is important for students to recognize that the result can be bad if they violate the hidden curriculum rules, and no matter what, they will have to figure out what to do next. Examples might include explaining that they didn't know about the rules/expectations and promising NOT to do it again, apologizing, and looking for more mature things to do.

Step 4: Take data using the Daily Data Tracker by counting the number of self-regulation strategies each student generates. Encourage students to list at least two strategies and then ask them to tell you what number on their 3- or 5-point Modulation Chart (see pages 184-185) they would assign to each situation. If they have two strategies for each situation, there would be a total of 6 data points. If students can identify the number situation on their modulation chart and explain their choice, give them 1 additional point for each of the situations, for a total of 9 points.

What Would Happen If I Didn't Know That ...
Hidden Curriculum and Self-Regulation

What Would Happen If I Didn't Know That ...	Consequences	I Would Regulate My Behavior By Doing This ...
By the time boys get to be 8 or 10 years old, they stop hugging each other and shake hands or do a "high-five." (from a boy's point of view)		
Was 17 years old and still liked to talk about Barbie dolls to my classmates (from a girl's point of view)		
Said a "bad" word in front of a teacher or maybe my grandma. (anybody)		

References – Hidden Curriculum and ASD

Garnett, K. (1984). Some of the problems students encounter in learning a school's hidden curriculum. *International Journal of Reading, Writing, and Learning Disabilities, 1*, 5-10.

Hemmings, A. (2000). The hidden corridor curriculum. *The High School Journal, 83*, 1-10.

Myles, B. S., Trautman, M., & Schelvan, R. (2004). *The hidden curriculum: Practical solutions for understanding unstated rules in social situations.* Shawnee Mission, KS: Autism Asperger Publishing Company.

Have you surveyed your students lately?

Chapter 5

Sensory Processing and ASD

Many students with ASD have sensory processing challenges. This means that **their nervous system cannot efficiently detect and use the sensory information that their bodies are receiving and sending.** When this occurs, they can become mildly uncomfortable, or they can become so uncomfortable that it feels as if they are in extreme physical pain. When students with ASD are unaware of their senses general and how they affect their bodies when sensory processing doesn't go smoothly, the result often appears to be behavioral challenges. One example may be a student tipping her chair back on two legs, facing backwards, or tapping her feet. When you hear someone say, "I don't know what triggered the incident," "it just happened," or "one minute he was fine, the next minute he was screaming and trying to leave the classroom," the cause may be traced back to a sensory processing problem.

The purpose of the activities in this section is to increase sensory awareness among individuals with ASD and help them to become environmental detectives, learning how to adapt and compensate for any physical discomfort they may feel. Ideally, such awareness will reduce occurrences of students getting upset or acting out behaviorally because they will be aware of the origin of the problem more quickly.

According to researchers, sensory processing allows for four different profiles when responding to sensory input. The patterns of response reflect both the individual's threshold – the levels of input required by the nervous system before it responds – and his self-regulation techniques – the range of methods used to respond to tasks or environmental stimuli.

One of the ways that students may attempt to regulate their behavior is through the use of active strategies such as twirling in circles, swinging intensely, or using a punching bag. Students may also regulate their behavior by controlling the amount or type of sensory input they receive. If the student is more passive in his self-regulation techniques (putting head down, lying in dark or quiet room, listening to music), he may appear to be less concerned about his surroundings or be unaffected by sensory input such as someone calling his name or walking into the room. This may mirror lethargy or an emotional "shut down," so consult a professional for support in making an accurate assessment of the cause. The thresholds and self-regulation strategies are measured in relation to each other to arrive at the following processing pattern types:

- **Low Registration:** These are the students who appear to be uninterested in or unexcited about and oblivious of the environment around them. The theory is that most of the activities in their daily routines do not include enough intensity to reach a threshold that engages and makes them active.
- **Sensation Seeking:** Students who exhibit this pattern need or prefer additional sensory experiences, so they actively seek them out to satisfy their needs. They appear to be excitable, busy, and constantly engaging in some type of activity even when socially inappropriate.
- **Sensory Sensitivity:** Extremely active like their sensory-seeking peers, these students are also distractible and tend to verbalize their sensory experiences. They choose this passive strategy of verbalizing rather than taking more active steps such as removing themselves from the environment.
- **Sensory Avoiding:** These students have low thresholds; so in order to mediate unpleasant sensory experiences, they use active strategies such as swinging, walking, or seeking deep pressure.

You may see any one or more of these patterns in your students – to a milder degree, you may detect some of them in yourself. If students have not already had a sensory evaluation by an occupational therapist or a professional trained in sensory integration, observe for evidence of sensory challenges or ask caregivers for more information, and seek a referral for appropriate services if necessary. If students have not been identified for formal occupational therapy, the activities in this section can only enhance their ability to self-regulate behaviors in the future.

REMEMBER: Only an occupational therapist or a professional trained in sensory integration is qualified to identify sensory deficits and recommend specific interventions or programming to comprehensively address a student's therapeutic needs.

NOTE: Students do not always exhibit the same response patterns to sensory input. They may alternate to accommodate their needs as they vary from one situation to the next throughout the day.

Life Examples

Suzanne

Situation: Suzanne's mother took her daughter to the doctor for a check-up to ask about why she always seems to be "quietly hanging around" and "not interested in playing with her siblings or the neighbors." Her mother continued to say that when she tries to make Suzanne go outside with the kids, she "just curls up in a chair or on her bed and hides."

Student Response: While it is possible that Suzanne is anxious or shy about playing with others, it is also possible that her situation is an example of low registration. Suzanne may have a very high threshold for sensory input and, therefore, is not receiving enough sensory input to become more active. A referral for evaluation by an occupational therapist might be in order.

Keisha

Situation: Keisha's teacher has reported consistent behavioral difficulties during lunch. Typically, Keisha can get through the food line, but by the time she is seated at her assigned table, she is always getting out of her seat, talking too loudly, asking to go to the bathroom and bumping into her classmates. Other students do not want to sit with her, and she is being labeled as a "trouble maker" by cafeteria staff.

Student Response: Keisha's situation is an example of sensory-seeking behavior. She may have auditory sensory challenges that make the noise of the cafeteria physically uncomfortable to her. She may also have difficulty with her olfactory or smell sense, and the multitude of smells blending together in the cafeteria may be making her feel sick. As a result, Keisha's behavior may be an attempt to seek enough sensory stimulation to help her calm herself. It would be helpful to have her evaluated for sensory challenges, but you can test the theory by having her eat with a couple of friends in a counselor's office or in another classroom or office in the school to see if she behaves differently than in the cafeteria.

Kevin

Situation: Kevin's mother reports that every time he wears tube socks, he complains of "pebbles or bumps" in his socks. When he can no longer tolerate the feeling, he rips off his shoes and socks, looking for the offending item. He often refuses to wear socks at all.

Student Response: Kevin's situation is an example of being sensory sensitive. His sense of touch may be challenged, making him overly sensitive to the feel of specific clothing. He may appear to be oppositional in an effort to avoid wearing things that are uncomfortable for him, or his behavior may escalate when he can't find relief from the discomfort. His mother might try turning his socks inside out or buying a different style of sock (for example, seamless sock) to find something that is physically tolerable for him.

Zach

Situation: Zach does well in middle school except for his shop class where his teacher reports that he often gets out of his seat and paces around the shop and out in the hallway. The teacher fears for Zach's safety because of the machines and other materials in the shop and a lack of supervision in the hallway.

Student Response: Zach's situation is an example of sensory avoiding behavior. It is possible that the bright lights required in the shop environment are causing visual discomfort for Zach. It is also possible that his ears are bothered by the machines or that his nose is offended by the smell of paints or chemicals. He might be pacing in order to calm himself and might need to wear sunglasses or a cap for his eyes or use ear plugs to maintain a comfortable level for his ears.

Impact on Development of Other Skills

Sensory processing challenges may inhibit academic progress because the student is not able to compensate for the discomfort sufficiently to focus on learning. There is also a direct connection between sensory processing deficits and the ability to self-regulate behaviors, and all of this can influence the student's ability to successfully function in daily life activities. For students with ASD, direct instruction in topics such as sensory awareness will support successful development of self-regulation skills.

NOTE: The icons used to represent each of the senses on pages 139-153 are referred to as Sensory Gang members. They are used with the permission of Autism Asperger Publishing Company, www.asperger.net

 Strategic Bomb Alerts! A Ticket to Perseveration Station Strategic Bomb would be very appropriate support while teaching sensory awareness.

Measurable Goals for Learning
Sensory Processing

Each of the goals below can be used for an IEP, behavior intervention plan (BIP) or treatment plan based on the student's current programming. The goals are listed in order of skill complexity and correspond with the sequential ordering of the lesson plans for each section. In most cases, there are several lesson plans for satisfying each goal.

Only the goal is included in the ECLIPSE Model. Criteria for measurement, such as "8 out of 10 times weekly for 6 consecutive weeks," must be added by each student's team or primary teacher, as appropriate.

NOTE: As long as all seven senses are highlighted during the activities, it does not matter in which order they are introduced.

---

1. Jake will learn about his seven senses and be able to distinguish them from each other.
2. Jake will list at least three positive and three negative ways that his senses affect his behaviors.
3. Jake will demonstrate at least three ways to compensate for the maladaptive behaviors that occur because of sensory processing deficits.
4. Jake will recognize and identify a minimum of five daily life situations that are affected by his senses.

Learning About Each of Your Senses

 Objective: To increase student understanding of the bodily senses and their influence on physical comfort or behaviors.

 Required Materials: One copy of a Sensory Gang member profile (for example, olfactory) and the handout, "Identifying Our Senses," magazines, newspapers, and pictures of different types of environments; scissors, envelopes; laminator and laminating film (optional)

 Required Prep Time: 20 minutes to make copies of all Sensory Gang members the first time; after that, 10 minutes

Required Activity Time: 30 minutes

 Embed Factor: 3

 Brief Overview: This activity gives a general overview of the seven senses and allows students to identify sensory characteristics. You will need to perform the activity for each of the seven senses; however, it is not necessary to complete all of them in one session. It is preferable to cover one or two senses at a time and review periodically to help maintain awareness of all of the senses.

Step 1: Gather pictures of different environments from magazine, posters, newspapers, or any other source where you can find interesting things. Try to find examples of as many different types of environments as possible. You might want to look for pictures of things like restaurants, field of flowers, activity on city streets or sidewalks, or even the inside of a factory or office building. Choose one of the seven sensory profiles (for example, olfactory) to review with the whole group. Make copies of the profile and corresponding character sheets for each student. Have the students cut out each of the Sensory Gang members on the character sheets that you are studying – if possible, laminate for protection. Provide students with envelopes to keep their characters organized.

Step 2: Start out by having students choose different environments that would make the Sensory Gang character feel good. As they make their choices, ask them to share why they made a particular choice. In other words, ask them "What about that environment would make the Sensory Gang member feel good?"

Step 3: Ask each of the students to identify pictures of environments that would make their own sense of _____ feel good and have them explain why.

Step 4: Repeat Step 2, but this time ask students to find pictures of environments that would make the Sensory Gang member feel uncomfortable or bad. Have them explain their decisions to the rest of the group.

Step 5: Repeat Step 3, except have students identify pictures that would make their own sense feel uncomfortable or bad. Be sure to focus on what physical clues their body is using to tell them what is wrong.

Step 6: Once you have completed this activity with all seven Sensory Gang characters, have each student identify each of the Sensory Gang members and explain what they affect. Take data using the Daily Data Tracker. Students should be able to identify at least five of seven senses correctly.

Extra Extra! Be sure to collect the envelopes of Sensory Gang members at the end of the lesson so they are available for future lessons.

Identifying Our Senses!

	Sight/Vision
	Hearing/Auditory
	Smell/Olfactory
	Taste/Gustatory
	Balance/Vestibular
	Proprioceptive
	Touch/Nerve

Take a Look at Your Eyes!!!

Scientific Name: Sight or Vision

Special Talent: Seeing as far or close as you need so that you have enough information about your environment to help you make decisions.

Preferred Habitat: Rooms or places that aren't too bright or too dark.

Potentially Unfriendly Environments: Flashing or flickering lights, very bright sun or fluorescent lights, and chemicals that burn.

You Can Help Me If You ...: Give me sunglasses when it is bright, give me time to adjust when it is dark, and protect me when playing sports.

Hear All About Your Ears!!!

Scientific Name: Auditory

Special Talent: Detecting noises in your environment that may give clues to how you should behave or that are just plain fun to listen to.

Preferred Habitat: Good music that isn't too loud, people laughing, most sounds that are not extreme.

Potentially Unfriendly Environments: Fire sirens, lawn mowers, loud concerts, cafeterias, and sporting events.

You can help me if you ...: Keep me clean and free from obstructions and protect me if you know things will be loud where you are going to be.

Get to Know Your Nose!!!

Scientific Name: Olfactory

Special Talent: Identifying smells that are in your environment and then sending your brain messages to help you decide how to respond them.

Preferred Habitat: Kitchens where cookies are baking, flower gardens, fresh laundry warm from the dryer, and chocolate factories!

Potentially Unfriendly Environments: Garbage dumps, rotten eggs, fish, dirty socks, and chemical cleaners.

You can help me if you ...: Keep me clear, don't block me when I sneeze, and rub me with lotion when I am red and sore.

Get a Taste of Your Tastes!!!

Scientific Name: Gustatory

Special Talent: Helping you decide which foods taste good and are safe to eat.

Preferred Habitat: Eating or drinking foods that are healthy, as spicy as you like, and not too hot or too cold.

Potentially Unfriendly Environments: Too much salt or spice, extremely hot or cold food, and dangerous chemicals.

You can help me if you ...: Check the temperature of your food before you take a bite. If I tell you something tastes bad or strange, listen to me because I might be warning you of danger.

The Basics of Balance!

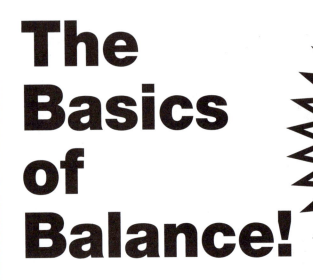

Scientific Name: Vestibular

Special Talent: Helping your body maintain a sense of balance and coordination.

Preferred Habitat: Pretty much any place that feels stable or movement that I have time to adjust to.

Potentially Unfriendly Environments: Crazy amusement rides, spinning too much, and sometimes ear troubles make me dizzy.

You can help me if you ...: Give me a chance to help your body adjust to movement and use visual reminders to help me understand what your body should do.

Meet the Master of Moving!!!

Scientific Name: Proprioceptive

Special Talent: Helping your body coordinate movement without you even thinking about it!

Preferred Habitat: I go everywhere you do, but you may not know it!

Potentially Unfriendly Environments: You will know I am having trouble if you are feeling awkward or clumsy, riding a skateboard or bike around corners, or climbing lots of stairs.

You can help me if you …: Practice movements that are challenging to you in classes like karate or yoga, maybe add music and move to the rhythm or look for visual clues that tell your brain how to respond.

Get in Touch With What You Feel!!!

Scientific Name: Tactile

Special Talent: Helping your body decide what feels comfortable to you.

Preferred Habitat: Soft clothes, sometimes clothes that are loose, and sometimes clothes that are tight, foods that feel good in your mouth.

Potentially Unfriendly Environments: Clothes, food, art supplies, and personal grooming activities that make me feel more discomfort than I can tolerate.

You can help me if you ...: Try listening to the signals I send you, because it will give you clues on how to behave and keep you safe and comfortable.

Becoming a Sensory Detective

Objective: To practice identifying the connection between human senses and physical comfort or behaviors.

Required Materials: Student envelopes with complete set of Sensory Gang members for each

Required Prep Time: 10 minutes

Required Activity Time: 30 minutes

Embed Factor: 3

Brief Overview: Students need to practice making the connection between their senses and how they influence behaviors. By exploring the classroom or outdoor environments and matching each of the Sensory Gang characters to potential environmental influences, students will begin to generalize their awareness of the environmental influences on their behaviors. These lessons help to build the fundamental skills of self-regulation.

Step 1: Give students their envelopes with the Sensory Gang characters. Ask them to place Sensory Gang characters on items in the room where they think the sense would be helpful. For instance, if there is a window in the room, they could choose the vision character, or they could choose proprioception to help sit in a chair.

Step 2: Have students explain their choices to the whole group and then ask them to gather up their characters and put them back in their envelopes.

Step 3: Repeat Steps 1 and 2. However, this time ask students to place the Sensory Gang characters on items where they would be most uncomfortable; for example, the auditory or hearing character could be placed near the fire alarm.

Step 4: Repeat Steps 1-3 using an outdoor or community environment.

Step 5: Take data using the Daily Data Tracker for each student on how many characters he or she successfully placed during each step. That would equal a total of 28 placements (comfortable/uncomfortable for two settings times seven senses). As long as students can give an appropriate explanation for their choices, the placement should be counted as correct.

Sensory Treasure Hunt

Objective: To give students an opportunity to problem solve and identify their senses as they actively work their way through a series of steps.

Required Materials: One set of Sensory Gang members for each team to find. Create clues for each of the senses that are specific to the environment where you are having the hunt. Create one set of clues for each team and color code clues so that teams can be assigned to follow a specific color throughout the hunt. For example, if there is a flower garden in your outdoor play space, you could make a clue for the olfactory/nasal sense that reads "Follow this sense to a place that grows all summer long." If there are music instruments in the room, you could have clue for auditory/hearing that says, "Playing with me will bring you lovely sounds." Other examples might include:

1. "You will need this sense if you are eating lunch in this room." (gustatory, olfactory)
2. "This sense will help you get through the obstacle course in this room." (proprioceptive or vestibular)
3. "You will need this sense if the bells are ringing and it is time for class." (auditory)
4. "If you have paint on your hands, you will definitely be using this sense." (tactile)
5. "When you use this sense in your classroom, things will seem very clear." (visual)

Required Prep Time: 30 minutes

Required Activity Time: 45-60 minutes

Embed Factor: 2

Brief Overview: This fun activity is designed to give students a chance to interpret clues about each of the senses while they are completing a treasure hunt. They will have to use some group problem-solving skills and self-regulation, so you may want to do this more than once and change the clues as students develop more skills.

Step 1: Place the Sensory Gang characters wherever they belong to satisfy your clues. Divide students into teams of two or three. Assign colors to each team and distribute the first corresponding clue. Give the teams 15-20 minutes to find all seven characters, depending on the difficulty of the clue and the age of the students.

Step 2: When all teams have completed the hunt, have the entire group come together and talk about which of the characters were hard to find and which ones were easy. Ask students to generate ideas for other spots in the environment where they could place each sensory gang character.

Step 3: Take data using the Daily Data Tracker by having each student identify at least three ways in which each of the senses could be influenced by the environment around them.

Senses to the Rescue!

Objective: To identify the ways that our bodies can signal physical discomfort or danger.

Required Materials: White board or chalkboard; paper and pencils for each student

Required Prep Time: 15 minutes

Required Activity Time: 30-45 minutes, depending on the size of the group

Embed Factor: 3

Brief Overview: The purpose of this activity is to help students determine how their senses can affect how they feel in a given circumstance. For instance, if they are at a picnic and it is hot outside, the itchy feeling around their shirt collar might be due to the excessive heat. Their sense of touch is warning them that they are too hot and that they need to take action to make themselves feel better – cooler.

Step 1: Read the six scenarios below to the group, one at a time. Have students determine which senses might send distress signals and what action they can take to help make themselves feel better. Have them identify the sense by name, and then ask them to give functional examples of how to mediate the situation. The possibilities for correct answers are almost endless, so ask for explanations from students to demonstrate functional understanding of the situation. Be sure that all seven senses are covered during the conversation.

1. Being on a long car trip. (*proprioceptive, visual*)
2. Being at the elephant compound at a zoo. (*olfactory*)
3. Being in a classroom with fluorescent lights. (*visual, proprioceptive*)
4. Going to a kennel. (*auditory, olfactory*)
5. Swinging. (*vestibular, proprioceptive*)
6. Eating oatmeal or mashed potatoes, wearing fuzzy or soft sweatshirts, or itchy mittens. (*tactile, olfactory*)

Step 2: Give students each a chance to declare a "Sensory Emergency" and create their own scenarios for the rest of the group to identify the challenged senses and how to make the situation better. Explain to the students that a "Sensory Emergency" is when they are so physically uncomfortable that they can't stand the situation any longer. It may be a time when their behaviors are inappropriate, or they may need their modulation charts to help regulate their behaviors. It is an all out disaster, and it will be different for each of them. Encourage them to think of places or activities that bother them (for example, using finger paints, going to loud assemblies, eating certain foods). Be sure to have students generate strategies to compensate for the discomfort the challenged sense was caused.

> *Don't forget to remind students that one strategy they can always use is to seek help from a parent or a teacher and to make teacher and parents aware of their sensory challenges.*

Step 3: Take data using the Daily Data Tracker by giving each student a situation where sensory challenges would influence behaviors. Ask them to identify the senses involved and suggest functional steps they can take to improve the circumstances. Be sure to give a scenario that highlights at least three of the senses and ask for at least three strategies. That will yield a total of 6 data points, 3 for identifying senses and 3 for strategies. Students should be able to identify all of the data points correctly at this point.

Tasting Sensation

Objective: To explore various concepts associated with the sense of taste.

Required Materials: A variety of snacks and foods that are easy to prepare

Required Prep Time: 30-60 minutes, depending on how much food is prepared in advance

Required Activity Time: 15 minutes for the first part of the activity and 45-60 minutes for the eating!

Embed Factor: 1

Brief Overview: By tasting a variety of types of foods, students will learn to identify concepts such as sweet and sour and to express their preferences for one taste over another. This activity requires some advance planning, so be sure to read the directions thoroughly and schedule your time accordingly.

NOTE: Be sure to determine any food allergies that students may have before beginning the lesson.

Step 1: Ask students to identify types of foods that they would like to try or favorite foods that they would like others to try. Keep food items simple so you are not preparing a complicated meal. Encourage the group to choose snack, salad, or desert-type items. Make a list of one item for each student.

Step 2: Announce the date of the next session to caregivers and explain that students are exploring their sense of taste. Ask if families could donate some of the food that their student identified. If this is not possible, have the students help you prepare a small amount of the food prior to the group session. Be sure to bring a couple of quick, simple foods to make sure that there is enough variety. Students should be able to identify them as sweet, salty, spicy, sour, etc. You can make a party out of the activity, or create more of a laboratory atmosphere with stations for testing each food type.

Step 3: Serve the food buffet style so that students have a chance to taste as many of the foods as they are willing to try. Allow the group to enjoy the food and the companionship for a reasonable period of time.

Step 4: Have students take turns identifying the foods that they liked and disliked. They should be able to explain their choices. Be sure to remind them that it is O.K. to dislike a food because everyone's sense of taste is different. Do NOT force anybody to eat anything he or she dislikes.

Step 5: No data are taken for this activity. However, each student should be able to successfully express his or her preferences. The goal is for students to become more aware of their likes and dislikes and find effective ways to express themselves.

Touch Testing

Objective: To develop students' ability to identify and express their preferences using the sense of touch.

Required Materials: At least one interesting or unusual thing to feel/touch for each student set out on tables or desk tops. Handout, "Touch Testing! Tester Checklist," for each student; pencils for each student

Required Prep Time: 30 minutes

Required Activity Time: 15 minutes for the first part of the activity

Embed Factor: 1

Brief Overview: Similar to Tasting Sensation, this activity is designed to help students identify their likes and dislikes and to express their preference effectively. This requires some advance planning. Encourage students to be creative in their choices for touch experimentation.

Step 1: Have students brainstorm things that they would like to experiment with by touching. Examples include cold noodles, play dough, finger paints, mud, fuzzy towels, soft pillows, or clothing. Make a list of all of the suggestions and schedule the touch testing for the next group session.

Step 2: Distribute the Touch Testing! Tester Checklist and give each student a chance to go through the line touching and experimenting with each of the items. Remind them to wash their hands after they have touched everything. Then ask them to complete their checklist.

Step 3: When everyone has completed the touch testing, gather the group for a discussion of what each of the items felt like. Ask students to vote on which was the best item to touch and which was the worst. Be certain that each student explains at least one or two of their personal preferences to the group. Remind the group that these are personal preferences based on their personal senses and that, therefore, there are no wrong answers.

Step 4: As for Tasting Sensation, there are no data to take for this activity. Each student should be able to successfully express his or her preferences. The goal is for students to become more aware of their likes and dislikes and to find effective ways to express themselves.

Touch Testing!

Tester Checklist

Items I Touched	Did I Like It?	Why or Why Not?

NOTE: For students who have trouble writing, feel free to modify this activity by completing the "Items I Touched" column for them or giving them picture icons to use instead of writing.

References – Sensory Processing and ASD

Anzalone, M., Williamson, M., & Gordon, G. (2000). Sensory processing and motor performance in autism spectrum disorders. In A. Wetherby & B. Prizant (Eds.), *Autism spectrum disorders: A transactional developmental perspective* (pp. 143-166). Baltimore: Brookes Publishing.

Baranek, G. (2002). Efficacy of sensory and motor interventions for children with autism. *Journal of Autism and Developmental Disorders, 32,* 397-422.

Dunn, W. (2001). The sensations of everyday life: Empirical, theoretical, and pragmatic considerations, from the 2001 Eleanor Clarke Slagle Lecture. *American Journal of Occupational Therapy, 55,* 608-620.

Dunn, W., Saiter, J., & Rinner, L. (2002). Asperger Syndrome and sensory processing: A conceptual model and guidance for intervention planning. *Focus on Autism and Other Developmental Disabilities, 17*(3), 172-185.

Gal, E., Cermak, S., & Ben-Sasson, A. (2007). Sensory processing disorders in children with autism: Nature, assessment, and intervention. In R. Gabriels & D. Hill (Eds.), *Growing up with* autism*: Working with school-age children and adolescents* (pp. 95-123). New York: Guilford Press.

Keane, E. (2004) Autism: The heart of the disorder? Sensory processing and social engagement – Illustrations from autobiographical accounts and selected research findings. *Australian Journal of Early Studenthood, 29,* 8.

Myles, B. S., Dunn, W., & Orr, S. (2002). Sensory processing issues associated with Asperger syndrome: a preliminary investigation. *American Journal of Occupational Therapy, 56,* 97-102.

Myles, B. S., Hagiwara, T., Dunn, W., Rinner, L., Reese, M., Huggins, A., & Becker, S. (2004). Sensory issues in students with Asperger Syndrome and autism. *Education and Training in Developmental Disabilities, 39*(4), 283-290.

Taylay-Ongan, A., & Wood, K. (2000). Unusual sensory sensitivities in autism: A possible crossroads. *International Journal of Disability, Development and Education, 47,* 201.

Have you surveyed your students lately?

Chapter 6

Self-Regulation, Modulation, and ASD

By definition, self-regulation refers to a systematic effort to direct one's thoughts, feelings, and actions toward attaining one's goals. The goals we are talking about here are not outwardly directed, such as the goal of becoming a black belt in karate. Instead, they are covert goals like "understanding the problem" or "thinking of a solution," focused directly at managing our own behavior. **Self-regulation is the art of maintaining enough control over our own physical behaviors to generate and implement a socially acceptable response to the situation we are presented with.** While there are many things that may cause you to need to self-regulate your behaviors, one good possibility is that sensory processing deficits are making it difficult for you to do so. Research showing a connection between sensory processing and self-regulation of behavior is a recent but growing addition to the scientific literature.

For many individuals with ASD, self-regulation is a challenge in everyday life. Students who have difficulty in this area can appear impulsive in their responses, quick to act with little or no thought process beforehand, disruptive, rude, or even aggressive. For these students, there is a VERY short window of time for them to (a) assess their situation through the attribution process using the parameters of internal/external, controllable/uncontrollable and stable/unstable, (b) generate and evaluate alternative solutions, and (c) select and implement the chosen solution. That is a lot to do for anyone, not counting all of the other cognitive or social challenges that influence the time and control needed to do this successfully. Let's look at an example.

Casey knows that after lunch each day he goes to the sensory room for break before he returns to class. He says that the activity makes him feel good and that he is more successful in class because of it. On this day, when Casey went to the sensory room, he found a note on the door saying the room was closed for painting. This left him standing in the hallway trying to decide how to handle his disappointment and what to do next. If he is successful in self-regulating his behavior, he might realize that it is a temporary situation and ask to go another area where he can take a break instead of getting upset. If, on the other hand, he is not so successful, he could very quickly become angry and disruptive, and his response might get him in trouble.

One of the significant areas of concern within the realm of self-regulation is the skill of modulating our responses. Modulation is the "volume button" on our behaviors. Not surprisingly, responses to emotional reactions or social situations are the most challenging to modulate. In other words, when a youngster with ASD is faced with troubling social or emotional circumstances, she is likely to overreact. As you will see in the Life Examples, the tendency to overreact makes individuals with ASD likely targets for bullying and the focus of disciplinary attention.

Our ability to self-regulate our behavior varies on any given day even if we are presented with the same challenging situations over again. With all of this in mind, the activities in this section will help students recognize personal goals that foster successful self-regulation.

Life Examples

Will

Situation: Will, 16, was sent to the office for a loud outburst in class. His teacher reported that he "just started pounding his desk and yelling at another student in front of him." The other student had "no idea" of why he would be so upset and denied any involvement in the situation.

Student Response: In reality, before the "outburst," Will's classmate was whispering to him that he was a "stupid jerk" because he had trouble with math. Even though Will told him twice to stop, the student did it one more time, and eventually Will could no longer control his behaviors. There were no consequences for the other student because Will is a known "behavior problem." So not only does Will get sent to the principal's office, he also feels great anger that nobody believes him.

Sam

Situation: Sam, 12, likes to attend Boy Scouts. However, he has difficulty at outdoor summer activities because he does not tolerate heat well. Last week he was asked to leave the meeting early because he was rude to other students and the Scout master.

Student Response: Sam was physically uncomfortable from the heat – his shirt felt soggy and itchy around his collar. Not recognizing his physical discomfort as the source of his agitation, Sam snapped at people around him even though they had nothing to do with his troubles.

Samantha

Situation: Samantha, 11, has had persistent trouble riding the bus home from school this year. The bus driver regularly complains that Samantha refuses to stay in her seat, and he is concerned that her safety is in jeopardy. The driver has tried assigning Samantha to different seats in the bus, but her behaviors do not change. As a result, he has accused Samantha of being rude and disrespectful by disobeying him.

Student Response: Samantha may not have enough self-control to regulate her ability to stay in one seat for any length of time. She can repeat the rules for riding the bus and explains that she "has no idea" why she can't sit still. This confuses her parents and the principal because "if she can tell us what she is supposed to do, she should be able to do it and must be choosing not to." Their assessment of the situation would logically lead them to what might be a negative consequence, such as loss of bus riding privileges for Samantha when, in reality, she might benefit from support from an occupational therapist to maintain appropriate behaviors for longer periods of time.

Impact on Development of Other Skills

Self-regulation directly impacts every activity we engage in. For example, learning is impacted when students are distracted by their fidgety behaviors and their focus in not on the task at hand. In addition to learning, social interaction is influenced greatly if a person cannot behave in ways that conform to social expectations. There are few things more annoying to an adult caregiver, educator, or community service provider than when students are not able to control their "impulsive" behaviors. School and community placement opportunities will be limited to the facilities or organizations that are equipped with the knowledge and resources to manage the student's current behaviors.

All of this is complicated by the fact that every situation, caregiver, or professional carries a different set of behavioral expectations that are not immediately obvious to the individual with ASD. One example would be an older student who occasionally swears at home because his parents don't mind, but then gets a detention in school because he swore in front of the principal. (The section on hidden curriculum discusses how to support the development of awareness of social expectations in more depth.)

 Strategic Bomb Alerts! A Ticket to Perseveration Station or a Smart Card Strategic Bomb would be very appropriate support while teaching self-regulation or modulation.

Measurable Goals for Learning
Self-Regulation and Modulation

Each of the goals below can be used for an IEP or treatment plan based on the student's current programming. The goals are listed in order of skill complexity and correspond to the sequential ordering of the lesson plans for each section. In most cases, there are several lesson plans for satisfying each goal.

The goal is included in the ECLIPSE Model. Criteria for measurement, such as "8 out of 10 times weekly for 6 consecutive weeks," must be added by each student's team or primary teacher, as appropriate.

1. Jack will improve his ability to self-regulate his behaviors by identifying physical cues that indicate his behaviors are escalating.
2. Jack will learn the concept of modulating his behavior by balancing situations with responses using the 3- or 5-Point Modulation Chart.
3. Jack will identify situations that differentiate self-regulation from modulation.
4. Jack will demonstrate an awareness of at least three different strategies to self-regulate his behaviors during challenging social interactions.

What Is Self-Regulation and Why Do We Do It?

 Objective: To provide students with an opportunity to learn about multiple concepts associated with self-regulating their own behaviors.

 Required Materials: Chalkboard and chalk or a dry-erase board and markers

 Required Prep Time: 10 minutes

Required Activity Time: 30 minutes

 Embed Factor: 3

 Brief Overview: Students with ASD may find the physical act of self-regulating challenging due to sensory processing deficits or a general lack of awareness of their behaviors. This lesson is an overview designed to stimulate group conversation or activity. Encourage students to form their own definition of self-regulation so that it is functional to them during everyday circumstances.

Step 1: Discuss the difference between regulating our behavior and inhibiting our behavior. *Inhibition* is the ability to stop or restrain ourselves from performing a behavior. It is the proverbial "on/off" button. *Regulation* is how we control or measure the amount or type of behaviors we demonstrate, sort of like the "volume control." Be sure that students are clear about the differences before moving to the next step. An example of regulation might be standing completely still in a game of freeze tag while an example of regulation might be walking away from a bully that calls you a name instead of punching him in the face.

Step 2: Write the word "self-regulate" on a chalk or white board. Ask each student to contribute one idea of what it means to self-regulate his or her behavior. Examples include not yelling during a fight with parents or siblings, stopping conversations that are escalating out of control, whispering in a library, not petting the dog or cat too hard, or obeying speed limits when driving. Prompt or encourage the discussion by periodically offering suggestions if students are struggling. List as many examples as possible, or for students who have more trouble generating novel ideas, put some ideas on the board and ask students to help you explain why or how they would self-regulate in that situation.

Step 3: Ask students to list reasons why it is important to demonstrate our behaviors in acceptable and effective ways. Examples include not wanting to break rules or laws, trying to be socially acceptable in specific situation, or following the steps of a process that helps us reach our goals.

Step 4: Discuss the consequences of not being able to self-regulate our behaviors successfully. Be sure that each student contributes at least one idea. Examples include being asked to leave a theater or library because of making excessive noise or receiving a ticket for speeding.

Step 5: No data are taken for this introductory lesson. The purpose is to give students a safe environment for identifying and sharing their ideas and challenges regarding self-regulating their behavior.

Getting to Know Myself – What Makes Me Happy, Sad, and Mad?

Objective: To improve students' awareness of situations that require them to self-regulate their behaviors.

Required Materials: Handout, "Getting to Know Myself – What Makes Me Happy, Sad, and Mad?," for each student

Required Prep Time: 10 minutes

Require Activity Time: 30 minutes

Embed Factor: 5

Brief Overview: The first step in learning to self-regulate our behaviors is to look at what situations make up happy, sad, and mad. It is a basic, concrete way to help students identify potential problems BEFORE they occur. All too often, individuals with ASD get caught in circumstances that they know would upset them if they could just "see it coming." This activity is designed to start building that awareness. Encourage students to talk freely and support each other. Perhaps they will even make some new discoveries!

Step 1: Distribute the handout, "Getting to Know Myself – What Makes Me Happy, Sad, and Mad?," to each student. Use brainstorming to generate a group conversation about answers to each question that students may have in common.

Step 2: After 10-15 minutes, ask students to list at least three things for each column if they can. This should not take more than 5-10 minutes.

Step 3: When everyone in the group has completed his list, ask for volunteers to share a couple of their answers. Remind students that their answers are personal, so there are no "right" or "wrong" answers.

Step 4: Take data using the Daily Data Tracker on the number of personal answers that the students were able to list on their sheets. Students should be able to list at least three items for each of the three categories making a total of nine items minimum.

Getting to Know Myself – What Makes Me Happy, Sad, and Mad?

Directions: List at least three ideas for each column, if you can.

What Makes Me Happy?	What Makes Me Sad?	What Makes Me Mad?

Keeping a Balance

Objective: To review the concept of balancing as an introduction to modulation of behavior.

Required Materials: Small kitchen, bath, or science scales (option: two bath scales); a bag of small items to be weighed (the number of scales and toys will vary based on availability and the number of students in the group); alternative: see-saw

Required Prep Time: 15 minutes

Required Activity Time: 30 minutes

Embed Factor: 4

Brief Overview: Introduce modulating responses by having students practice balancing concrete items using scales, or see-saws if you have a playground outside. The idea is to provide a visual representation of keeping a balance between the situations we are faced with in everyday life and the responses that we choose to deal with them.

Step 1: Set up kitchen scale, small science scale, or two bath scales side by side and a bag of things to weigh (small toys, candies, or whatever is handy).

Step 2: Divide students into pairs or small groups and give each a random selection of items to weigh.

Step 3: Instruct the group to pick what they think is the heaviest item and put it on one side of the scale. They should see the other side go up and realize that the scale is clearly not balanced.

Step 4: Have students add one item at a time until they two sides of the scale balance evenly. (If using two bath scales, add times until both scales read the same.)

Step 5: Let students experiment with balancing all the different items. Tell them to choose which of the items that they used to balance were the most unusual. For instance, one pair of students may find that a roll of adhesive tape weighs the same as 10 pencils.

Step 6: After all students have had a chance to experiment and balance several items, gather the group to discuss any unusual items they used to create balance. Ask them to tell you whether or not they thought balancing items was difficult. Emphasize that having too much on one side of the scale will not let the scale balance. Most important, students should understand the concept of balance in a concrete, functional way. This lesson will serve as experiential preparation for future lessons that focus on balancing social situations and the responses to them.

Step 7: No data are taken for this introductory activity. There will be opportunities to test learning of modulation later.

Balance and Modulation – Putting Things in Order

 Objective: To practice rank ordering and matching several items at once.

 Required Materials: Handout, "Balancing Animals," for each student; chalkboard and chalk or dry-erase board and markers

 Required Prep Time: 20 minutes

Required Activity Time: 30 minutes

 Embed Factor: 3

 Brief Overview: This activity allows students to begin the process of rank ordering or assigning degrees of intensity, importance, etc., to items or situations in the world around them. We will practice the skill using a set of concrete concepts such as animals to maximize learning of the process. Once students are proficient with the process, we move on to using it with real-life scenarios that build awareness of self-regulation skills.

Step 1: Cut out the 20 animal names in the handout.

Step 2: Draw two columns on a chalk or white board, and down the left side write the numbers 1-5.

Step 3: Randomly assign numbers to the first 10 animal cards based on the animal's size. Number 1 would be the smallest animals of the group, and number 5 would designate the largest. You should end up with two columns of animal names that are in no way balanced or matching.

Step 4: Ask for a volunteer to come up to the board and reorder one side of the scale so that they are in order from smallest to largest. This illustrates the process of identifying degrees of size. We will follow the same process when we assign degrees of importance or severity to daily life situations.

Step 5: Ask for a second volunteer to complete the second column to match the first. This student will have to prioritize the size of the animals while also being certain that the sizes are balanced with those in the opposite column. In other words, the scale must be prioritized from smallest to largest vertically and also be balanced from left to right. For instance, a duck and a crow might be matched as similarly sized animals in one row, but they would certainly be smaller or at a lower number on the scale than a goat or a camel.

Step 6: After the second volunteer has completed her column, ask the rest of the group for feedback about whether or not the two columns are ordered and balanced correctly. If everyone is sure that they are okay, you are ready to move on to the next phase.

Step 7: Take one of the animal names in the second set and insert it in place of one of the other animals already on the board. Make sure to put the animal in the wrong spot, such as matching the dog with a turtle or hamster.

Step 8: Ask the group if what you did is correct. Students should realize that it is not. Allow one of the students to rearrange it in the proper size order. Continue this process with new volunteers each time, until the entire first set of animals has been replaced with the second set and is correctly ordered and balanced.

Step 9: Take data using the Daily Data Tracker by randomly choosing 10 animal cards for each student and asking them to order the cards based on size while also balancing them with the opposite column. Count the number of animal names correctly ordered by size (vertically) in both columns. That would be a maximum of 10 points. Then count the number of correctly matched pairs (horizontally), which would be another 5 points, for a total of 15 points. Students should successfully obtain at least 12 points for this to be considered a learned skill.

HAMSTER

TURTLE

PARROT

MONKEY

GOAT

FROG

GUINEA PIG

CROW

SLOTH

DOG

CHICKEN

PIG

ZEBRA

BUFFALO

MOOSE

Balance and Modulation Using the Modulation Chart

 Objective: To develop an individualized modulation chart for each student.

 Required Materials: Chalkboard and chalk; dry-erase board, or flipchart, and markers; handouts for each student, "My Modulation Chart" – both the 3- and the 5-point version

 Required Prep Time: 10 minutes

 Required Activity Time: 30 minutes

Embed Factor: 6

 Brief Overview: This lesson is designed to teach students to identify challenging situations, assign a degree of severity to them, and then identify appropriate responses for each level of severity. By using a chart format that they can keep as a reference, students have a visual reminder to help support the development of self-regulation and modulation of their own behavior. The ultimate goal is for students to numerically quantify the severity of any given situation and then select a response that is numerically balanced with that situation.

Step 1: Have each student think of as many upsetting or challenging situations as they can. Draw a Modulation Chart on a chalkboard, white board, or flip chart to look like the handout. The goal is to assign a degree of severity to each of the situations that students identify. Explain that situations listed in the number "1" box are things that they consider to be mildly upsetting or easily resolved. As they progress through blocks 2, 3, 4 and 5, the situations become more intense or severe in nature. If the students have trouble generating ideas, offer suggestions of situations that you know are troubling or ask parents to send a short list of ideas from home.

Extra Extra! The object is for each student to become comfortable identifying degrees of severity, so it is their responsibility to choose items for each block without influence from parents, caregivers, or professionals. As students call out their ideas, write them in the situation column of the chart at whatever level of the chart they assign.

Use the 3-point Modulation Chart with younger or more severely challenged students and the 5-point chart with all others. Once the students with 3-point charts become proficient in their use, transition them to a 5-point chart to further build skills of differentiation and prioritization.

Step 2: Give students a Modulation Chart and ask them to complete the Situation column alone or with a partner. Be ready to help brainstorm if necessary.

Step 3: When students have completed the column listing situations and assigning severity to each, have them complete the next column, which identifies what their first or natural response would be for each situation. The purpose of this column is to visually recognize the responses students may be choosing without much thought or self-regulation involved. Be sure to create an atmosphere where the students feel comfortable sharing honest answers, even if not socially appropriate.

Step 4: Once students are satisfied that they have filled in the Situation and My First Response columns to the best of their ability, have them fill in the last column, a more positive response. Be prepared to initiate a conversation with all of the students to brainstorm ideas for each of the degrees of severity.

Extra Extra! People with ASD have trouble forming abstract ideas in their heads and shifting from one idea to another. Using a chart as a visual reminder can help. The chart serves as a personal reference tool to help students select appropriate responses during stressful or upsetting situations. If possible, laminate or make copies of each student's chart so that they will last and be available for home, school, and group use. Consistent use of the chart will help students successfully self-regulate or modulate their behaviors before inappropriate behavior occurs.

Step 5: Instruct other adults to ask students what level they are on as soon as they see a potentially volatile situation developing. Once students have identified the level of severity, ask them what level of response they are demonstrating to focus their attention on the importance of balancing the two numbers. Reward students for successfully balancing situations and giving appropriate responses.

Extra Extra! Successful implementation of this intervention depends heavily on the willingness of adults around each student to prompt identification of difficult situations. Students will need to practice identifying the severity of the situation they are facing and then use the chart as a reminder for balanced, appropriate responses.

Step 6: Use the Modulation Chart as a behavior management strategy for group sessions. Have students find a place to keep their charts, or if everyone agrees, post them on a bulletin board or tape them to a wall for future reference. ONLY do this if everyone agrees, because some of the information on the chart may be personal, causing students to be uncomfortable sharing it.

Extra Extra! Successful implementation means that students will work to achieve a numerically defined balance between the situations they face and the responses they choose. Remind students that it won't always work as well as they would like, but that with time and practice most of them will be quite good at it.

Step 7: Using the Daily Data Tracker, data may be taken by counting the number of times that students demonstrate the use of the Modulation Chart successfully at each group meeting. Be sure to give students enough time to practice the skill before beginning data collection.

My Modulation Chart

How Serious Is It?	Situation	My First Response	A More Appropriate Response
1			
2			
3			

My Modulation Chart

How Serious Is It?	Situation	My First Response	A More Appropriate Response
1			
2			
3			
4			
5			

Balance and Modulation
Using the Modulation Chart and Real-Life Situations

 Objective: To apply the rank-ordering process from the previous lessons to real-life situations.

 Required Materials: Handout, "Balancing Situations and Strategies"; chalkboard and chalk or white board and markers

 Required Prep Time: 15 minutes

Required Activity Time: 30 minutes

 Embed Factor: 7

 Brief Overview: This activity is similar to Balancing and Modulation - Using the Modulation Chart, except that we will now use specific real-life situations. If the students mastered the concept of rank ordering the animals by size, they should be able to generalize that skill to real-life situations that are relevant to them. They may need some help getting away from ranking everything at the extreme ends of the chart (either a 1 or 5) and identifying other levels of intensity or severity in between.

Step 1: Cut out the 10 real-life situations and 10 possible strategies from "Balancing Situations and Strategies."

Step 2: Draw two columns on a chalk or white board, and down the left side write the numbers 1-5.

Step 3: Take the first set of five real-life situation cards and five possible strategy cards and randomly assign them to the numbers. Number 1 would be the least challenging situation and 5 would be the most challenging. You should end up with two columns of situations and strategies that are in no way balanced or matched.

Step 4: Ask for a volunteer to come to the board and reorder the situation side of the scale so that items are in order from least to most challenging. This illustrates the process of identifying degrees of importance or severity. Remember that by using real-life situations and strategies, the order may be different for each student based on his or her personal preferences.

Step 5: Have the same student reorder the five possible strategies so that they balance each real-life situation. The result should be the student's own chart, ordered by degree of severity (modulation) and then balanced from the situation to the response, using the numerical values of 1-5 (self-regulation).

Step 6: Ask each of the students to complete the activity on the board. Be sure to re-inforce the idea that everyone's answers might be slightly different and that as long as students can give reasonable explanations for their choices, they should be considered acceptable.

Remember that everyone's threshold for tolerance is different! So don't argue with where students choose to rank their situations. Students must feel entitled to their own opinion. Over time, ideally, they will shift their perceptions of the situations and rank them differently. This is a developmental skill that will evolve as the students mature.

Step 7: Take data using the Daily Data Tracker by counting the number of situations that are reasonably prioritized from 1-5. That would be a maximum of 5 points. Then count the number of reasonably matched strategies for each situation, which would be another 5 points, for a total of 10 points. Students should successfully achieve at least 8 points to be considered as having learned the skill.

Balancing Situations and Strategies – Strategies

BRING NEXT TIME

ASK FOR HELP LOOKING

ASK WHAT TO EXPECT NEXT

BRING THINGS TO KEEP BUSY

SIT IN BACK OF ROOM

Balancing Situations and Strategies – Strategies

TAKE BREAK

GET UP EARLIER

ASK WHAT THE RULES ARE

CALL VETERINARIAN

PLAY WITH SOMETHING ELSE

Balancing Situations and Strategies – Situations

SUBSTITUTE TEACHER

LOSE VIDEO GAME

LOUD ASSEMBLY

CHANGE IN PLANS

LONG CAR RIDE

Balancing Situations and Strategies – Situations

MISS BUS

FIGHT WITH SIBLING

SICK PET

FORGET HOMEWORK

LOST TOY

Keeping Track of Yourself! Using Personal Modulation Trackers

Objective: To generalize the skill of self-monitoring self-regulation of behaviors.

Required Materials: Blank Personal Modulation Tracker for each student at the beginning of each day/session; pens or pencils

Required Prep Time: 15 minutes

Required Activity Time: 1 minute for each Modulation Tracker Moment attempted throughout the day

Embed Factor: 10!

Brief Overview: This lesson is designed to help reinforce the transfer of responsibility for self-regulating behaviors to the students and to help them generalize the ability to self-monitor throughout the day in different environments. By recording their progress at intermittent points during the day, students will have created their own visual record of their self-regulation attempts. Most students quickly begin to focus on improving their ability to stay balanced after using the Personal Modulation Trackers regularly.

Step 1: Give each student a Personal Modulation Tracker and ask them to fill in their name and the date. Explain that during the session you will announce a Modulation Tracker Moment. This means that they should stop what they are doing and assign the numbers 1-5 or 1-3, depending on which chart they are using, to the situation ("How Serious Is it?") and their response ("How Am I Responding?"). Then they should answer "yes" or "no" to the question "Am I Balanced?"

Step 2: You can announce up to 10 Modulation Tracker Moments during any given session. At the end of the session, ask the students to add up the number of times they answered "yes" to "Am I Balanced?" and write the number in the box at the bottom of the Personal Modulation Tracker.

Step 3: Take data using the Daily Data Tracker by recording the number of times students report being balanced through the use of their Modulation Charts throughout the day.

My Personal Modulation Tracker

Name: _____   Date: _____

Situation Number	How Serious Is It?	How Am I Responding?	Am I Balanced?
1			
2			
3			
4			
5			
6			
7			
8			
9			
10			

My Personal Modulation Tracker

Name: _____   Date: _____

Situation Number	How Serious Is It?	How Am I Responding?	Am I Balanced?
1			
2			
3			
4			
5			
6			
7			
8			
9			
10			

Name That Goal!

 Objective: To identify appropriate behavioral responses to everyday situations.

 Required Materials: Handout, "Name That Goal! Game Clues"

 Required Prep Time: 20 minutes

Required Activity Time: 30-45 minutes, depending on the size of the group

 Embed Factor: 6

 Brief Overview: The purpose of this *Jeopardy*-style game is to allow students to use clues about a situation to identify a relevant self-regulation goal. Given that self-regulation goals are inwardly directed, the answers to the quiz questions will be things like "What is sitting still?" "What is not interrupting?" or "What is waiting my turn?" There may be more than one correct answer, so use your judgment and allow for a little flexibility as long as the answers are logical or fit the context of the situation. Encourage students to think of anything that they can do to help control their behavior and/or make the situation better. If the students are younger, their answers may include more physical actions and responses than verbal responses. With age and practice, they will likely move from describing physical actions to describing their thought processes.

Step 1: Ask students if they have seen the television show called *Jeopardy*. Tell them that in this lesson, they will need to answer the clues with a question just like in the game *Jeopardy*. One example might be "What is sitting still?"

Step 2: Have the students sit anywhere they are comfortable as long as they are together. Explain that they must raise their hand to answer and that you will call on them. If the answer is out of the realm of possibility, there is no penalty or discussion. Simply say, "Not quite," and call on someone else.

Step 3: Read each of the 10 clues on pages 193-194 with the group. You can pretend to do the TV announcer voice to make it more exciting if you like. Tell students that they are free to raise their hand as soon as you have read the entire clue and they think they have an answer.

Step 4: Make sure that each of the students has an opportunity to answer at least one of the questions. After you have completed all 10 clues provided, you may want to make up clues that you know would be relevant or challenging to individual students.

Step 5: Once all of the clues have been identified correctly, have students gather for a discussion of the different clues and how difficult they were to identify. See if you can recognize any group commonalities and draw attention to them. Perhaps several students will think "not swearing" is the hardest thing to do when the situation is frustrating or that "asking for a break" is an easy goal to identify.

Step 6: Create a scenario for each student that you know is a behavioral challenge for him or her. For instance, if you know a student has trouble on the bus, you may want to give a clue like: "When I ride the bus, there is very little room, and it is loud. The driver says I have to stay still, but I can't stand when other people touch me, even by accident. What little steps can I take to change my behavior so that the bus ride is easier for me?" Possible answers might include asking for a seat alone, bringing ear plugs, reminding myself that the ride is short, or asking to use a Walkman or some other personal music player.

Step 7: Take data using the Daily Data Tracker. After you explain the individualized situations to students, ask them to list five different goals they might set to make the situation better. They should be able to list at least four. The number of possible answers is endless, so as long as an answer makes sense for a given situation, count it as correct.

Name That Goal!
Game Clues

1. My mom and I go to the grocery store after school once a week. I am stuck going, because Mom says that I am too young to stay home by myself. A lot of the time we end up in an argument because I don't want to stay with her the whole time. The truth is that I get tired of standing up so much and have a tough time not bumping into people around us in the aisles. **Possible answers: What is … "Ask to sit down somewhere and wait, ask to push the cart so I can lean on it, or tell Mom it wears me out to follow her."**

2. When I am in gym class at school, the teacher blows her whistle and yells directions, but I am never sure if she is talking to me or not. Sometimes she gets angry at me because she says I didn't listen and makes me sit on the side. I wish I could be better at gym, but I can never tell what is going to happen next, and it makes me nervous, so I have trouble thinking fast enough. **Possible answers: What is … "Ask the gym teacher to call my name when she needs me or stay close enough to the teacher to hear what she says."**

3. After school I like to play my video games because it gives me a chance to relax from all of the stuff I had to do at school. My mom wants me to do homework first, but when I try to do that, my brain feels like it's going to explode. Mom thinks I am trying to get out of doing my homework, but if I had time to relax first, I wouldn't mind doing it right before dinner. **Possible answers: What is … "Explain that I just need to relax for a little while, pick a time to do my homework and DO IT, or tell Mom that my brain feels tired and as soon as I rest it gets better and I can do the work easily."**

4. Last week I got in trouble at school because I pushed a girl in the hallway. She made me mad, and I did it before I could think of anything else to do. The girl told me that I was "stupid" because I buy my lunch every day. I don't think it is stupid to buy lunch, because I really like the food. I didn't know what else to do, so I pushed her. **Possible answers: What is … "Walk away, tell her to mind her own business, or tell a teacher."**

5. I usually like to have dinner with my family at holidays, but this time I had a meltdown. Dad and Grandma thought I was upset because they tried to make me eat more turkey, but that wasn't it at all. Grandma called me a "bad girl," and it made me angry. The truth is that I didn't want to sit at the table any more because my tights were making my legs itch. **Possible answers: What is … "Explain that my tights are making me itch, ask politely to be excused, ask to take the tights off."**

6. My brother and I were playing in the family room when he pushed the restart button on our video game. I grabbed his controller and threw it across the room, so he cried. My mom blamed me because I threw the controller, but I think she should have punished my brother. He only turns off the game when he is losing and wants to keep me from winning. **Possible answers: What is … "Not play video games with my brother, walk away instead of throwing the controller, or call Mom for help."**

7. There are so many books about Rome in our school library that I like to just sit on the floor and read them. The other day the librarian told my teacher I was disrespectful because I left a pile of books on the floor. Part of the problem was that I was so excited to read about Rome that I just kept looking for more information. I didn't want to put the books back in the wrong place, so I left them. **Possible answers: What is … "Take one book at a time and put it back before I get another, take one or two books to a table, or ask for help putting them back in the right place."**

8. My family went on a car trip last weekend to the state park. It was two hours away, and I got bored in the car. I kept asking how much longer it would be before we got there, and my parents got so angry that I wasn't allowed to hike my favorite trail when we finally got there. That punishment made no sense to me, because I always have trouble on long car rides, I can't stand sitting still that long. **Possible answers: What is … "Ask to bring toys, music, or books to keep me busy, bring a pillow and rest, or try to keep track of time so I know how much longer the trip will be."**

9. Every time we are in group and we go outside, I get in trouble because I would rather look at the bugs and things in nature than play the games we are supposed to be doing. The group leader says I have to stop. I get angry and sometimes yell at him. He says it is disrespectful not to do what he says, but I am not hurting anything. I just want to look for bugs. **Possible answers: What is … "Ask to split the time between the game and bug hunting, explain that playing group games outside makes me hot and sweaty, tell Mom or Dad that I need help resolving the problem."**

10. I got invited to a birthday party that included going to see a new cartoon movie. It was fun, but I got in trouble for not staying in my seat. They called my parents to come and get me. When my parents came, I got upset and cried because I wanted to stay with my friends. The problem was that the movie was so loud that I was getting a headache, and I thought if I left for a few minutes it would go away. **Possible answers: What is … "Don't go to the movies, but meet the group for the rest of the party, tell my friends that I am going to the bathroom because my head hurts, or hold my ears with my fingers for a while."**

Self-Regulating – PURE NONSENSE!

Objective: To provide students with an opportunity to demonstrate functional self-regulation skills successfully.

Required Materials: 2 boxes of tissues; bags of cotton balls or paper napkins; and Modulation Charts for each student.

Required Prep Time: 10 minutes

Required Activity Time: 30 minutes

Embed Factor: 3 or as often as you have time for

Brief Overview: This section of the curriculum has been hard work for students, so this activity is meant to reinforce the idea of self-regulation and modulation through a silly game. You can have the students bring a box of tissues from home or buy some inexpensive ones and bring them. When the game is over, gather them up and store them in a big bag for the next time you play. The activity requires students to recognize possible escalations in their excitement as the game progresses. Be prepared to laugh and have FUN!

Step 1: Divide students into small groups, no larger than four or five members each. Have each group sit in a circle on the floor. Students should be at least an arm's length from each other.

Step 2: Explain the rules: (a) you may not lift your backside off of the floor, and (b) you may not touch another person. Students who break rules are asked to sit out for one round of the game. Ask students to identify where they are on the scale of 1-5 of their Modulation Chart. Once they have decided (most should be a 1), dump a large pile of tissues, cotton balls, or paper napkins in the middle of the circles and tell the groups they are to have a tissue battle.

Step 3: When you say, "GO!" they are allowed to reach in and grab tissues to throw at other students. They should quickly realize they need to "ball up" the tissues to be effective. They are free to team up and target each other.

Step 4: Time the rounds for 3 minutes at a time. When stopping, ask students to decide where they are on their Modulation Chart. They should recognize that they are escalating in excitement each time you ask them to assess their condition.

Step 5: After three to four rounds, have students clean up the tissues and save them for another day. Take a few minutes to discuss how students knew they were getting more excited each round. You are encouraging students to identify physical clues from their bodies that indicate growing excitement. Be sure to point out the connection to self-regulating their behaviors so they can stay in the game. They are achieving the goals of not touching others, staying focused on the game, and not getting so excited that they can no longer participate.

Step 6: There are no data to take on this activity. It is a fun way to practice all of the steps in self-regulation and modulation whenever you have a few free minutes. For such a silly idea, there are LOTS of benefits!

References – Self-Regulation

Laurent A., & Rubin E. (2004). Challenges in emotional regulation in Asperger syndrome and high-functioning autism. *Topics in Language Disorders*, *24*, 286-297, 316-322.

Lee, S., Simpson, R. L., & Shogren, K. A. (2007). Effects and implications of self-management for students with autism: A meta-analysis. *Focus on Autism and Other Developmental Disabilities, 22*, 2-13.

Myles, B. S., Dunn, W., & Orr, S. (2002). Sensory processing issues associated with Asperger syndrome: A preliminary investigation. *American Journal of Occupational Therapy, 56*, 97-102.

Nacewicz, B., Dalton, K., Johnstone, T., Long, M., McAuliff, E., Oakes, T., Alexander, A., & Davidson, R. (2006). Amygdala volume and nonverbal social impairment in adolescent and adult males with autism. *Archives of General Psychiatry, 63*, 1417-1428.

Schunk, D. H., & Zimmerman, B. J. (Eds.). (1994). *Self-regulation of learning and performance: Issues and educational applications.* Hillsdale, NJ: Lawrence Erlbaum Associates.

Whitman, T. (2004). *The development of autism: A self-regulatory perspective*. New York: Jessica Kingsley.

Wilkinson, L. A. (2005). Supporting the inclusion of a student with Asperger syndrome: A case study using conjoint behavioural consultation and self-management. *Educational Psychology in Practice, 21*, 307-332.

Wilkinson, L. A. (2008). Self-management strategies for students with high-functioning autism spectrum disorders. *Intervention in School and Clinic, 43,* 150-157.

Chapter 7

Data Collection and Record Keeping

This section includes data collection sheets and other record-keeping materials. The teacher checklist will keep you on the right track.

ECLIPSE Model Teacher Implementation Checklist Sample

Teacher or Group Leader Activities	Frequency of Activity	Date	Date	Date	Date	Date	Date	Date	Date	Date	Date	Date	Date
Distribute Permission Slips	Once Prior to Implementation												
Do Student Survey, What I Think About My Group!	Once Prior to Implementation and Monthly Thereafter												
Complete Any Standardized Preassessment Instruments	Once Prior to Implementation												
Do Baseline ECLIPSE Model Behavior Indicator Data Collection	Once a Day for 10 Days Prior to Implementation												
Choose up to Six ECLIPSE Model Goals for Each Student	Once Prior to Implementation, and as Often as Progress Dictates												
Use Five-Day ECLIPSE Model Behavior Indicator Data Collection	30 Days After Implementation, and Every Month Thereafter												
Introduce and Review ECLIPSE Model Lessons	Daily if Possible, or at Least 3 Times Weekly												
Complete ECLIPSE Model Implementation Record	Every Time a Lesson is Introduced or Reviewed												
Complete Any Standardized Post-Assessment Surveys	Once After Group or School Year Has Ended												
Have Students Write in Independence Journal	At Least Once Weekly												
Conduct Reality Checks	At Least 3 Times Weekly												
Use Self-Awareness Builders	Daily at The End of the Day												

ECLIPSE Model Teacher Implementation Checklist

Teacher or Group Leader Activities	Frequency of Activity	Date	Date	Date	Date	Date	Date	Date	Date	Date	Date	Date	Date

ECLIPSE Model Implementation Record

★ Star Indicates Embed Factor

Activity Name	Introduction Date	Review Trial 1	Review Trial 2	Review Trial 3	Review Trial 4	Review Trial 5	Review Trial 6	Review Trial 7	Review Trial 8	Review Trial 9	Review Trial 10
ATTRIBUTION RETRAINING											
Getting Started			★								
Attribution Retraining – Introducing the Concepts of Internal/External – Concrete					★						
Attribution Retraining – Introducing the Concepts of Internal/External Abstract									★		
Applying Attribution Retraining to Real-Life Scenarios											★
ABSTRACT THINKING											
Brainstorming							★				
Making Your Expectations Box	★										
Expectations Game						★					
Paint Me a Picture In My Head						★					
Identifying Details of an Abstract Concept					★						
SHIFT OR MENTAL FLEXIBILITY											
The Beginnings of Change				★							
The Sounds of Change			★								
No Perseveration Station, Please!					★						

ECLIPSE Model Implementation Record (Cont.)

★ Star Indicates Embed Factor

Activity Name	Introduction Date	Review Trial 1	Review Trial 2	Review Trial 3	Review Trial 4	Review Trial 5	Review Trial 6	Review Trial 7	Review Trial 8	Review Trial 9	Review Trial 10
THEORY OF MIND											
What Are They Thinking?				★							
Just the Facts, Please!			★								
Uncovering All the Facts #1			★								
Uncovering All the Facts #2			★								
Uncovering All the Facts #3			★								
Uncovering All the Facts #4			★								
Theory of Mind and Natural Consequences						★					
Theory of Mind in a Social Environment							★				
HIDDEN CURRICULUM											
Introduction to Hidden Curriculum			★								
Hidden Curriculum in a Social Environment							★				
Becoming a Hidden Curriculum Detective				★							
Keeping a Hidden Curriculum Diary					★						
Hidden Curriculum and Self-Regulation							★				

ECLIPSE Model Implementation Record (Cont.)

★ Star Indicates Embed Factor

Activity Name	Introduction Date	Review Trial 1	Review Trial 2	Review Trial 3	Review Trial 4	Review Trial 5	Review Trial 6	Review Trial 7	Review Trial 8	Review Trial 9	Review Trial 10
SENSORY											
Learning About Each of Your Senses				★							
Learning About Each of Your Senses				★							
Learning About Each of Your Senses				★							
Learning About Each of Your Senses				★							
Learning About Each of Your Senses				★							
Learning About Each of Your Senses				★							
Learning About Each of Your Senses				★							
Becoming a Sensory Detective				★							
Sensory Treasure Hunt			★								
Senses to the Rescue!				★							
Tasting Sensation		★									
Touch Testing		★									

★ Star Indicates Embed Factor

ECLIPSE Model Implementation Record (Cont.)

Activity Name	Introduction Date	Review Trial 1	Review Trial 2	Review Trial 3	Review Trial 4	Review Trial 5	Review Trial 6	Review Trial 7	Review Trial 8	Review Trial 9	Review Trial 10
SELF-REGULATION/MODULATION											
What Is Self-Regulation and Why Do We Do It?				★							
Getting to Know Myself – What Makes Me Happy, Sad, and Mad!						★					
Keeping a Balance					★						
Balance and Modulation – Putting It All in Order				★			★				
Balancing Situations Using the Modulation Chart							★				
Balance and Modulation – Using the Modulation Chart and Real-Life Situations								★			
Keeping Track of Yourself! Using Personal Modulation Trackers											★
Name That Goal!							★				
Self-Regulating – PURE NONSENSE				★							

ECLIPSE Model
Behavior Indicator Data Sheet Sample

Enter Number of Times Behaviors Occur Here

Enter Date Here

Student Name: SAMPLE

ECLIPSE Model Behavior Indicator	EXAMPLE 4/14/08	4/15/08	4/16/08	4/17/08	4/18/08	4/21/08	4/22/08	4/23/08	4/24/08	4/25/08	Total Number of Each Behavior
Verbally interrupts group activity, distracting others	3	4	2	5	3	3	5	4	4	4	37
Physically interrupts group activities, distracting others	1	0	1	2	1	1	3	1	0	2	13
Refuses to comply with directions	5	6	4	5	7	4	4	6	5	5	51
Overreacts to problem	3	5	3	2	3	4	3	2	4	4	33
Misunderstands others	2	4	4	3	5	4	4	5	3	3	37
Requires removal from class	0	0	0	0	1	0	1	0	0	1	3
Refuses to respect social boundaries	2	4	4	3	3	3	3	4	4	3	31
Resists transition to new activity	1	2	2	3	2	1	3	2	2	3	21
Willing to ask for help/ break prior to outburst	0	0	0	2	1	1	0	1	1	2	8
Attempts to help self or others problem solve	1	1	0	0	2	0	1	1	2	0	8
Staff Initials	SAM	SAM	SAM	SAM	SAM	SAM	SAM	SAM	SAM	SAM	SAM

ECLIPSE Model
Behavior Indicator Data Sheet

Student Name: _____

Enter Number of Times Behaviors Occur Here

Enter Date Here

ECLIPSE Model Behavior Indicator										Total Number of Each Behavior
Verbally interrupts group activity, distracting others										
Physically interrupts group activities, distracting others										
Refuses to comply with directions										
Overreacts to problem										
Misunderstands others										
Requires removal from class										
Refuses to respect social boundaries										
Resists transition to new activity										
Willing to ask for help/ break prior to outburst										
Attempts to help self or others problem solve										
Staff Initials										

207

ECLIPSE Model Behavior Indicator Monthly Summary and Trend Tracker Sample

Student Name: SAMPLE

ECLIPSE Model Behavior Indicator	Verbally interrupts group activity, distracting others	Physically interrupts group activity, distracting others	Refuses to comply with directions	Overreacts to problem	Misunderstands others	Requires removal from class	Refuses to respect social boundaries	Resists transition to new activity	Willing to ask for help/ break prior to outburst	Attempts to help self or others problem solve	Staff Initials
Month 1	41	8	52	68	53	6	41	59	7	11	SAM
Month 2	47	8	57	55	57	6	37	54	9	11	SAM
Month 3	38	6	51	49	51	4	34	55	14	16	SAM
Month 4	40	7	43	50	44	5	27	44	12	19	SAM
Month 5	32	5	38	39	41	3	22	40	17	22	SAM
Month 6	30	5	35	32	33	3	18	39	20	25	SAM
Month 7	22	4	31	25	29	4	15	32	28	26	SAM
Month 8	19	4	22	20	26	3	15	26	27	31	SAM
Month 9	15	3	18	19	22	2	12	23	30	34	SAM
Month10											
Month 11											
Month 12											

ECLIPSE Model Behavior Indicator Monthly Summary and Trend Tracker

Student Name: _____

ECLIPSE Model Behavior Indicator	Month 1	Month 2	Month 3	Month 4	Month 5	Month 6	Month 7	Month 8	Month 9	Month10	Month 11	Month 12
Verbally interrupts group activity, distracting others												
Physically interrupts group activity, distracting others												
Refuses to comply with directions												
Overreacts to problem												
Misunderstands others												
Requires removal from class												
Refuses to respect social boundaries												
Resists transition to new activity												
Willing to ask for help/ break prior to outburst												
Attempts to help self or others problem solve												
Staff Initials												

Instructions for Using the
What I Think About My Group! Survey

Use the "What I Think About My Group" survey before you begin the curriculum so that you have a baseline estimation of your students' impressions about the class or group. Then administer the survey once a month during the program so that you can track any improvements in students' perceptions about the class or group. Many students may not feel as positively as they did during the first month or two. This may indicate that they were struggling to acquire the new skills being introduced. If there is no improvement after two consecutive months, you may want to go back and review the appropriateness of the treatment or IEP goals.

What I Think About My Group!

Date completed: _____

Number of students in group: _____

Directions: Circle one answer for each of the questions below.

1. Do you have any friends in your class or group?   Yes   No   Don't Know

2. Do you participate in activities with
    other students in the class or group?   Yes   No   Don't Know

3. Do the other students in the group or class upset you?

1	2	3	4	5
Not At All	Sometimes	Yes, But I Can Deal With It	Enough to Make Me Feel Angry Myself	So Much That I Feel out of Control More Often Than I Like to Be

4. Would you like to have more
    friends in the group or class?   Yes   No   Don't Know

5. Does your teacher help you solve problems?

1	2	3	4	5
Never	Sometimes	Only When He/She Has the Time	Most of the Time He/She Is Helpful	Always! I Can Count on My Teacher to Help Me

6. Do you overreact to things around you?   Yes   No   Don't Know

7. How well do you control your behavior?

1	2	3	4	5
Not	A Little Bit	Only When I Am Calm and Happy	More Than the Others in My Group	Always! I Hardly Ever Lose Control

8. Do you get upset if you have to change activities before you are ready to?   Yes   No   Don't Know

9. Do the other students try to make you angry on purpose?   Yes   No   Don't Know

10. Do you like to be with the other students in the group or class?   Yes   No   Don't Know

ECLIPSE Model Abbreviated Universal Goal Tracking Sheet Sample

Student Name: SAMPLE

Goal	Required Data Benchmark Being Measured	Bench-mark and Date	Bench-mark and Date	Bench-mark and Date	Bench-mark and Date	Bench-mark and Date	Bench-mark and Date	Bench-mark and Date	Bench-mark and Date	Bench-mark and Date	Date Goal Completed
Mark will demonstrate at least five strategies for determining the hidden curriculum of a situation.	Number of strategies demonstrated.	1st 1/12/08	2nd and 3rd 1/31/08	4th 2/17/08	5th 3/12/08						3/12/08
Mark will identify a minimum of five daily life situations that are affected by his senses.											
Mark will identify details that can be grouped to form an abstract concept.											
Mark will identify at least five physical cues that indicate his behaviors are escalating.											
Mark will learn the concept of modulating his behavior by balancing situations with responses using a 5-point Modulation Chart.											
Mark will identify at least 10 different mental states that can be carried out by others.											
Staff Initials											SAM

ECLIPSE Model Abbreviated Universal Goal Tracking Sheet

Student Name: _____

Goal	Required Data Benchmark Being Measured	Bench-mark and Date	Bench-mark and Date	Bench-mark and Date	Bench-mark and Date	Bench-mark and Date	Bench-mark and Date	Bench-mark and Date	Bench-mark and Date	Date Goal Completed
Staff Initials										

ECLIPSE Model
Universal Goal Tracking Sheet

SAMPLE

Student Name: _____

Goal: Mark will demonstrate at least five strategies for determining the hidden curriculum of a situation.

What Is Being Measured? Number of demonstrated strategies for determining hidden curriculum.

Date of Activity	Lesson Name	Target Behavior	Number Correctly Performed	Goal Achieved? Yes/No	Staff Initials
1/12/08	Hidden curriculum in a social environment	Five demonstrated strategies	1	No	SAM
1/16/08	Becoming a hidden curriculum detective	Five demonstrated strategies	2	No	SAM
1/22/08	Review hidden curriculum in a social environment	Five demonstrated strategies	5	Yes	SAM

ECLIPSE Model
Universal Goal Tracking Sheet

Student Name: _____

Goal: _____

_____

What Is Being Measured? _____

Date of Activity	Lesson Name	Target Behavior	Number Correctly Performed	Goal Achieved? Yes/No	Staff Initials

My Personal Goal Tracker Sample

My Name: SAMPLE   Date: _____

What Is My Goal?	What am I measuring? (My Benchmark)	Bench-mark	Bench-mark	Bench-mark	Bench-mark	Bench-mark	Bench-mark	Bench-mark	Did I Meet Goal? Yes or No and Date
Mark will demonstrate at least five strategies for determining the hidden curriculum of a situation.	Number of strategies. Every time I learn a new strategy for identifying hidden curriculum, I will write it down.	Look for signs to read that have rules or info.	Ask people to explain what I need to do to fit in.	I can copy what others do as long as they aren't in trouble.	I can decide what group of people I am with and what they would do.	I can keep my diary to remember what I learn			YES! 1/25/08
Mark will identify a minimum of five daily life situations that are affected by his senses.	Number of daily life situations. Every time I identify a situation that is affected by my senses, I will write it down.								
Mark will identify details that can be grouped to form an abstract concept at least five times.	Number of abstract concepts. Every time I put the right details together to make an abstract concept, I will write it down.								
Mark will identify at least five physical clues that indicate his behaviors are escalating.	Number of physical clues that I am getting angry. Every time I identify a new physical clue, I will write it down.								
Mark will identify at least 10 different mental actions that can be carried out by others.	Number of mental actions that I can identify.								
Mark will learn the concept of modulating his behavior by balancing situations with responses using a Modulation scale	Number of times I use the Modulation Chart to balance situations and responses.								

My Personal Goal Tracker

My Name: _____   **Date:** _____

What Is My Goal?	What am I measuring? (My Benchmark)	Bench-mark	Bench-mark	Bench-mark	Bench-mark	Bench-mark	Bench-mark	Bench-mark	Bench-mark	Bench-mark	Did I Meet Goal? Yes or No and Date

Daily Data Tracker Sample

Student Name: John Smith   **Data:**   3/17/09

Lesson Name: Attribution Retraining: Introducing the Concepts of Internal and External (Concrete Items ONLY)

Review Trial Number: 3

Skill Being Measured	Number of Possible Points	Number of Actual Points Earned	Percentage Correct	Benchmark Achieved Yes/No?
Assigning 1 parameter of attribution to concrete concepts	5	3	60%	No

Daily Data Tracker

Student Name:_____ Data: _____

Lesson Name: _____

_____

Review Trial Number: _____

Skill Being Measured	Number of Possible Points	Number of Actual Points Earned	Percentage Correct	Benchmark Achieved Yes/No?

Appendix

Strategic Bombs – Perseveration Station

**ADMIT ONE
GOOD FOR ONE-WAY TRIP**

P

**PERSEVERATION
STATION**

At the absolute worst moment, when you are desperate for ideas and want to do the right thing, your brain completely freezes. You have no choice but to insist that you are right or refuse to move on to the next activity.

**ADMIT ONE
GOOD FOR ONE-WAY TRIP**

P

**PERSEVERATION
STATION**

At the absolute worst moment, when you are desperate for ideas and want to do the right thing, your brain completely freezes. You have no choice but to insist that you are right or refuse to move on to the next activity.

**ADMIT ONE
GOOD FOR ONE-WAY TRIP**

P

**PERSEVERATION
STATION**

At the absolute worst moment, when you are desperate for ideas and want to do the right thing, your brain completely freezes. You have no choice but to insist that you are right or refuse to move on to the next activity.

**ADMIT ONE
GOOD FOR ONE-WAY TRIP**

P

**PERSEVERATION
STATION**

At the absolute worst moment, when you are desperate for ideas and want to do the right thing, your brain completely freezes. You have no choice but to insist that you are right or refuse to move on to the next activity.

From Moyer, S., NHS Inc. (2009). *The ECLIPSE Model: Teaching Self-Regulation, Executive Function, Attribution, and Sensory Awareness to Students with Asperger Syndrome, High-Functioning Autism, and Related Disorders*. Shawnee Mission, KS: Autism Asperger Publishing Company; www.asperger.net. Used with permission.

Strategic Bombs – Perspective Pickle

Perspective Pickle

You are interacting with others and have determined that you thoroughly and accurately understand their thoughts, feelings, and intentions. You are ready to act but find no success.

Perspective Pickle

You are interacting with others and have determined that you thoroughly and accurately understand their thoughts, feelings, and intentions. You are ready to act but find no success.

Perspective Pickle

You are interacting with others and have determined that you thoroughly and accurately understand their thoughts, feelings, and intentions. You are ready to act but find no success.

Perspective Pickle

You are interacting with others and have determined that you thoroughly and accurately understand their thoughts, feelings, and intentions. You are ready to act but find no success.

Strategic Bombs – Smart Card

SMART CARD

In the event that all other conversational strategies fail during stressful interactions, you are allowed to top all other statements by declaring your unequaled giftedness and natural superiority.

SMART CARD

In the event that all other conversational strategies fail during stressful interactions, you are allowed to top all other statements by declaring your unequaled giftedness and natural superiority.

SMART CARD

In the event that all other conversational strategies fail during stressful interactions, you are allowed to top all other statements by declaring your unequaled giftedness and natural superiority.

SMART CARD

In the event that all other conversational strategies fail during stressful interactions, you are allowed to top all other statements by declaring your unequaled giftedness and natural superiority.

The First Step to Assessing the Circumstances

Internal

External

Conclusion: Some things are naturally part of us, some things are not.

From Moyer, S., NHS Inc. (2009). *The ECLIPSE Model: Teaching Self-Regulation, Executive Function, Attribution, and Sensory Awareness to Students with Asperger Syndrome, High-Functioning Autism, and Related Disorders*. Shawnee Mission, KS: Autism Asperger Publishing Company; www.asperger.net. Used with permission.

Another Step to Assessing the Circumstances

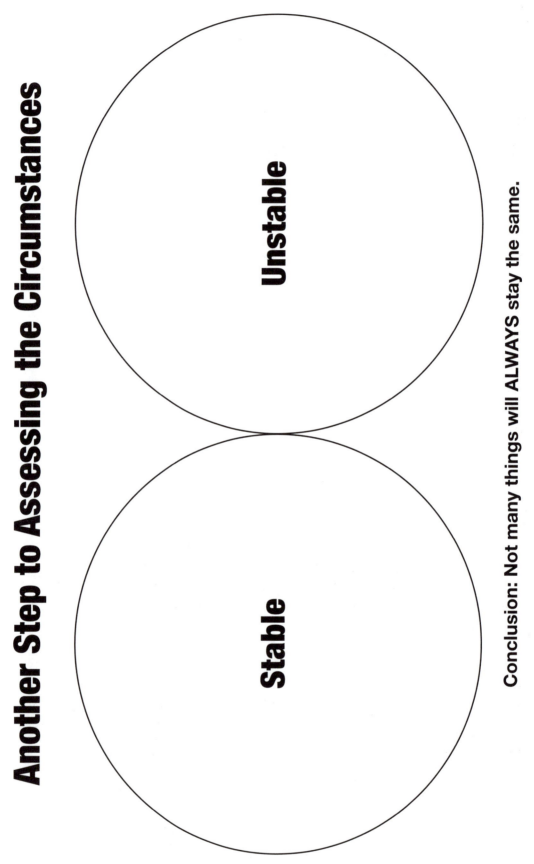

Unstable

Stable

Conclusion: Not many things will ALWAYS stay the same.

One Last Step to Assessing the Circumstances!

Uncontrollable

Controllable

Conclusion: We may have control over more things than we think!

Why Did This Happen to Me?

	Exactly What Happened?	Was It Internal or External to You?	Was It Stable or Unstable?	Was It Controllable or Uncontrollable?	Assessment or Attribution of the Cause or Motivation	Are You Motivated to Take Action and Improve the Situation?
At First Look						
On Second Thought						

From Moyer, S., NHS Inc. (2009). *The ECLIPSE Model: Teaching Self-Regulation, Executive Function, Attribution, and Sensory Awareness to Students with Asperger Syndrome, High-Functioning Autism, and Related Disorders*. Shawnee Mission, KS: Autism Asperger Publishing Company; www.asperger.net. Used with permission.

Brainstorming

Idea/Concept: Vacation

List as many ideas as you can think of about a vacation.

_____

_____

_____

_____

_____

_____

_____

_____

_____

_____

_____

_____

Brainstorming

Idea/Concept: Sports game

List as many ideas as you can think of about a sports game.

_____

_____

_____

_____

_____

_____

_____

_____

_____

_____

_____

_____

_____

Brainstorming

Idea/Concept: Restaurants

List as many ideas as you can think of about a restaurant.

_____

_____

_____

_____

_____

_____

_____

_____

_____

_____

_____

_____

_____

Brainstorming

Idea/Concept: Neighborhood

List as many ideas as you can think of about a neighborhood.

_____

_____

_____

_____

_____

_____

_____

_____

_____

_____

_____

_____

_____

_____

Brainstorming

Idea/Concept: Halloween

List as many ideas as you can think of about Halloween.

_____

_____

_____

_____

_____

_____

_____

_____

_____

_____

_____

_____

_____

Brainstorming

Problem Solving: Asking someone for a date
(Use this example wherever age appropriate.)

List as many ideas as you can think of about what to do if you want to ask someone out on a date.

_____

_____

_____

_____

_____

_____

_____

_____

_____

_____

_____

_____

Brainstorming

Problem Solving: Missing the bus to school

List as many ideas as you can think of about what to do if you miss the bus to school.

_____

_____

_____

_____

_____

_____

_____

_____

_____

_____

_____

From Moyer, S., NHS Inc. (2009). *The ECLIPSE Model: Teaching Self-Regulation, Executive Function, Attribution, and Sensory Awareness to Students with Asperger Syndrome, High-Functioning Autism, and Related Disorders*. Shawnee Mission, KS: Autism Asperger Publishing Company; www.asperger.net. Used with permission.

Brainstorming

Problem Solving: Brother or sister broke favorite Lego creation

List as many ideas as you can think of about what to do if your brother or sister broke your favorite Lego creation.

_____

_____

_____

_____

_____

_____

_____

_____

_____

_____

_____

_____

Brainstorming

Problem Solving: Needing a ride to work
(Use this example for students who are transition age.)

List as many ideas as you can think of about what to do if you need a ride to work.

_____

_____

_____

_____

_____

_____

_____

_____

_____

_____

_____

_____

Brainstorming

Problem Solving: Your computer died!

List as many ideas as you can think of about what to do if your computer dies.

_____

_____

_____

_____

_____

_____

_____

_____

_____

_____

_____

_____

_____

_____

From Moyer, S., NHS Inc. (2009). *The ECLIPSE Model: Teaching Self-Regulation, Executive Function, Attribution, and Sensory Awareness to Students with Asperger Syndrome, High-Functioning Autism, and Related Disorders*. Shawnee Mission, KS: Autism Asperger Publishing Company; www.asperger.net. Used with permission.

Concept: Summer Vacation

Camp	**Beaches**
Flowers	**Popsicles**
Grass	**Leopards**
Friends	**No School**

From Moyer, S., NHS Inc. (2009). *The ECLIPSE Model: Teaching Self-Regulation, Executive Function, Attribution, and Sensory Awareness to Students with Asperger Syndrome, High-Functioning Autism, and Related Disorders*. Shawnee Mission, KS: Autism Asperger Publishing Company; www.asperger.net. Used with permission.

Concept: Birthday Party

Ice Cream	**Dump Truck**
Cake	**Prizes**
Pinata	**Games**
Face Painting	**Music**

Concept: Classroom

Desks

Computers

Books

Cars

Chalkboard

Trash Can

Laundry

Pencils

From Moyer, S., NHS Inc. (2009). *The ECLIPSE Model: Teaching Self-Regulation, Executive Function, Attribution, and Sensory Awareness to Students with Asperger Syndrome, High-Functioning Autism, and Related Disorders.* Shawnee Mission, KS: Autism Asperger Publishing Company; www.asperger.net. Used with permission.

Concept: Pet Store

Hamsters	**Fish**
Bowls	**Pet Food**
Cages	**Beds**
Pet Toys	**Candles**

Concept: Holidays

Relatives	**Presents**
Trips	**Parties**
Microscope	**Food**
Long Car Ride	**Music**

From Moyer, S., NHS Inc. (2009). *The ECLIPSE Model: Teaching Self-Regulation, Executive Function, Attribution, and Sensory Awareness to Students with Asperger Syndrome, High-Functioning Autism, and Related Disorders.* Shawnee Mission, KS: Autism Asperger Publishing Company; www.asperger.net. Used with permission.

Concept: Visit to Dentist

Drills	**Bright Lights**
Floss	**Fake Teeth**
Mouthwash	**Mirror**
Receptionist	**Toothpaste**
Doctors	**Zebras**

Concept: Oceans

Boats	**Sharks**
Waves	**Sand**
Sea Weed	**Oil Wells**
Sting Rays	**Trash**
Coral	**Dogs**

Concept: Forests

Ticks	**Spiders**
Trees	**Moss**
Campers	**Rabbits**
Car Wash	**Streams**
Bears	**Birds**

Concept: Factory

Assembly Lines	**Boxes**
Noise	**Safety Goggles**
Lights	**Machines**
Time Clocks	**Beds**
Fork Lifts	**Trash Cans**

From Moyer, S., NHS Inc. (2009). *The ECLIPSE Model: Teaching Self-Regulation, Executive Function, Attribution, and Sensory Awareness to Students with Asperger Syndrome, High-Functioning Autism, and Related Disorders.* Shawnee Mission, KS: Autism Asperger Publishing Company; www.asperger.net. Used with permission.

Concept: Arctic Circle

Seals	**Reindeer**
Icebergs	**Cold**
Water	**Palm Trees**
Snow	**Walruses**
Polar Bears	**Whales**

From Moyer, S., NHS Inc. (2009). *The ECLIPSE Model: Teaching Self-Regulation, Executive Function, Attribution, and Sensory Awareness to Students with Asperger Syndrome, High-Functioning Autism, and Related Disorders.* Shawnee Mission, KS: Autism Asperger Publishing Company; www.asperger.net. Used with permission.

Identifying Details of an Abstract Concept

	"Must Have"	"Nice to Have"	"Don't Really Need"
Planting a garden			
Having a party			
Going camping			
Add your own here			
Add your own here			

From Moyer, S., NHS Inc. (2009). *The ECLIPSE Model: Teaching Self-Regulation, Executive Function, Attribution, and Sensory Awareness to Students with Asperger Syndrome, High-Functioning Autism, and Related Disorders.* Shawnee Mission, KS: Autism Asperger Publishing Company; www.asperger.net. Used with permission.

"What Are They Thinking?" Head Silhouette

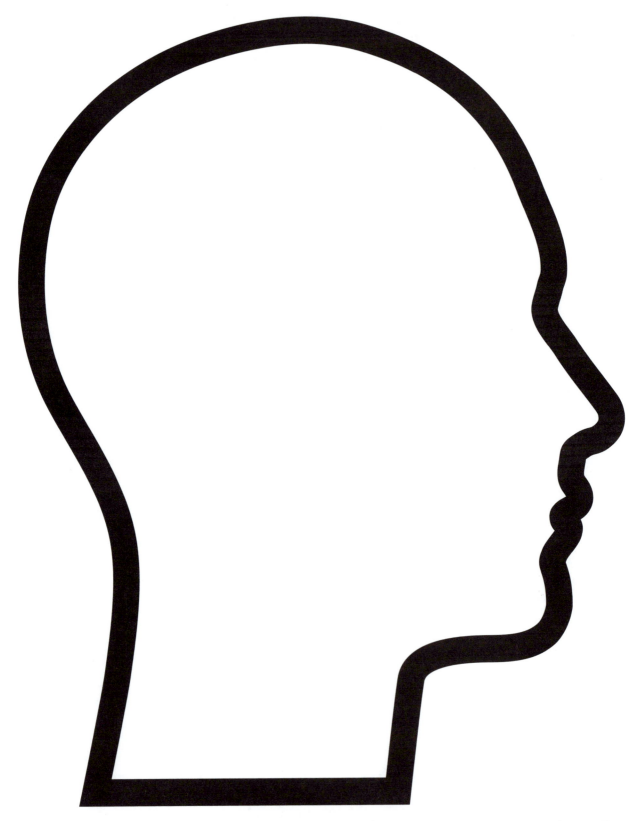

Uncovering All the Facts #1

Reporter's Name: _____

Subject's Name: _____

1. How do you spend your time at home?_____

    _____

    _____

    _____

2. What do you do on weekends?_____

    _____

    _____

    _____

3. Who are the people in your family? _____

    _____

    _____

    _____

4. What time of year do you like most? Why?_____

    _____

    _____

    _____

Uncovering All the Facts #2

Reporter's Name: _____

Subject's Name: _____

1. Are there any sports that you like to play or watch? If yes, please name them. _____

   _____

   _____

   _____

2. Can you tell me about the most interesting place that you have ever been? _____

   _____

   _____

   _____

3. Do you ever have to do something that you don't like? If yes, please explain. _____

   _____

   _____

   _____

4. Do you attend camps or hobby groups like Boy Scouts or youth groups? If yes,
   please name them. _____

   _____

   _____

Uncovering All the Facts #3

Reporter's Name: _____

Subject's Name: _____

1. What do you do when you meet new people? _____
   _____
   _____
   _____

2. Do you get scared by anything? If yes, please explain. _____
   _____
   _____
   _____

3. What kinds of things help you calm down? _____
   _____
   _____
   _____

4. What kinds of activities do you like to do with other people? _____
   _____
   _____
   _____

Uncovering All the Facts #4

Reporter's Name: _____

Subject's Name: _____

1. Where have you been on school field trips? _____

   _____

   _____

   _____

2. Tell me about your neighborhood. _____

   _____

   _____

   _____

3. Do you know what you would like to be when you grow up? If yes, please explain. ___

   _____

   _____

   _____

4. What is the most boring thing that you have ever had to do? _____

   _____

   _____

   _____

What Would Happen if I Didn't Know That ...

What Would Happen If I Didn't Know That ...	Consequences	I Would Regulate My Behavior By Doing This ...
... I should not talk about Grandma's stinky perfume in front of her.		
... I have to say "excuse me" if I bump into someone.		
... If I am having a party, I shouldn't talk about it in front of people who are not invited.		

From Moyer, S., NHS Inc. (2009). *The ECLIPSE Model: Teaching Self-Regulation, Executive Function, Attribution, and Sensory Awareness to Students with Asperger Syndrome, High-Functioning Autism, and Related Disorders*. Shawnee Mission, KS: Autism Asperger Publishing Company; www.asperger.net. Used with permission.

Diagnosing the Hidden Curriculum

Case (situation):

Symptoms or characteristics (what is happening?):

Strategies for diagnosing the situation (how to reveal theory of mind):

What is the recommended treatment (how should I behave)?

Hidden Curriculum Activity

Having Friends Over to Spend the Night

1. Your friends arrange to have enough blankets and pillows so everyone has his or her own, or ask to bring their own.

2. Usually, boys and girls don't spend the night at the same house unless they are family members.

3.

4.

5.

6.

7.

8.

9.

10.

11.

12.

13.

14.

15.

Hidden Curriculum Activity

Going to a Movie With Friends

1. Once the lights go down in the theater, it is not polite to talk during the movie.

2. Try to leave at least one seat between you and any person you don't know unless you don't have any choice (that is, there are no empty seats).

3.

4.

5.

6.

7.

8.

9.

10.

11.

12.

13.

14.

15.

Hidden Curriculum Activity

Eating at a Restaurant

1. Try to speak just loud enough for the people at your table to hear you and not loud enough for people at other tables to hear you.

2. If you taste something bad in your food, it is polite to quietly spit it into your napkin without making any comments about what you are doing.

3.

4.

5.

6.

7.

8.

9.

10.

11.

12.

13.

14.

15.

My Hidden Curriculum Diary

Directions: List at least two ideas for each category and bring to the next group session.

Age	
Place	
Male/Female	
People You Are With	
School	
Work	

What Would Happen If I Didn't Know That ...
Hidden Curriculum and Self-Regulation

What Would Happen If I Didn't Know That ...	Consequences	I Would Regulate My Behavior By Doing This ...
By the time boys get to be 8 or 10 years old, they stop hugging each other and shake hands or do a "high-five." (from a boy's point of view)		
Was 17 years old and still liked to talk about Barbie dolls to my classmates (from a girl's point of view)		
Said a "bad" word in front of a teacher or maybe my grandma. (anybody)		

From Moyer, S., NHS Inc. (2009). *The ECLIPSE Model: Teaching Self-Regulation, Executive Function, Attribution, and Sensory Awareness to Students with Asperger Syndrome, High-Functioning Autism, and Related Disorders*. Shawnee Mission, KS: Autism Asperger Publishing Company; www.asperger.net. Used with permission.

Identifying Our Senses!

	Sight/Vision
	Hearing/Auditory
	Smell/Olfactory
	Taste/Gustatory
	Balance/Vestibular
	Proprioceptive
	Touch/Nerve

Take a Look at Your Eyes!!!

Scientific Name: Sight or Vision

Special Talent: Seeing as far or close as you need so that you have enough information about your environment to help you make decisions.

Preferred Habitat: Rooms or places that aren't too bright or too dark.

Potentially Unfriendly Environments: Flashing or flickering lights, very bright sun or fluorescent lights, and chemicals that burn.

You Can Help Me If You ...: Give me sunglasses when it is bright, give me time to adjust when it is dark, and protect me when playing sports.

Hear All About Your Ears!!!

Scientific Name: Auditory

Special Talent: Detecting noises in your environment that may give clues to how you should behave or that are just plain fun to listen to.

Preferred Habitat: Good music that isn't too loud, people laughing, most sounds that are not extreme.

Potentially Unfriendly Environments: Fire sirens, lawn mowers, loud concerts, cafeterias, and sporting events.

You can help me if you …: Keep me clean and free from obstructions and protect me if you know things will be loud where you are going to be.

From Moyer, S., NHS Inc. (2009). *The ECLIPSE Model: Teaching Self-Regulation, Executive Function, Attribution, and Sensory Awareness to Students with Asperger Syndrome, High-Functioning Autism, and Related Disorders.* Shawnee Mission, KS: Autism Asperger Publishing Company; www.asperger.net. Used with permission.

Get to Know Your Nose!!!

Scientific Name: Olfactory

Special Talent: Identifying smells that are in your environment and then sending your brain messages to help you decide how to respond them.

Preferred Habitat: Kitchens where cookies are baking, flower gardens, fresh laundry warm from the dryer, and chocolate factories!

Potentially Unfriendly Environments: Garbage dumps, rotten eggs, fish, dirty socks, and chemical cleaners.

You can help me if you ...: Keep me clear, don't block me when I sneeze, and rub me with lotion when I am red and sore.

Get a Taste of Your Tastes!!!

Scientific Name: Gustatory

Special Talent: Helping you decide which foods taste good and are safe to eat.

Preferred Habitat: Eating or drinking foods that are healthy, as spicy as you like, and not too hot or too cold.

Potentially Unfriendly Environments: Too much salt or spice, extremely hot or cold food, and dangerous chemicals.

You can help me if you ...: Check the temperature of your food before you take a bite. If I tell you something tastes bad or strange, listen to me because I might be warning you of danger.

The Basics of Balance!

Scientific Name: Vestibular

Special Talent: Helping your body maintain a sense of balance and coordination.

Preferred Habitat: Pretty much any place that feels stable or movement that I have time to adjust to.

Potentially Unfriendly Environments: Crazy amusement rides, spinning too much, and sometimes ear troubles make me dizzy.

You can help me if you ...: Give me a chance to help your body adjust to movement and use visual reminders to help me understand what your body should do.

From Moyer, S., NHS Inc. (2009). *The ECLIPSE Model: Teaching Self-Regulation, Executive Function, Attribution, and Sensory Awareness to Students with Asperger Syndrome, High-Functioning Autism, and Related Disorders.* Shawnee Mission, KS: Autism Asperger Publishing Company; www.asperger.net. Used with permission.

Meet the Master of Moving!!!

Scientific Name: Proprioceptive

Special Talent: Helping your body coordinate movement without you even thinking about it!

Preferred Habitat: I go everywhere you do, but you may not know it!

Potentially Unfriendly Environments: You will know I am having trouble if you are feeling awkward or clumsy, riding a skateboard or bike around corners, or climbing lots of stairs.

You can help me if you ...: Practice movements that are challenging to you in classes like karate or yoga, maybe add music and move to the rhythm or look for visual clues that tell your brain how to respond.

From Moyer, S., NHS Inc. (2009). *The ECLIPSE Model: Teaching Self-Regulation, Executive Function, Attribution, and Sensory Awareness to Students with Asperger Syndrome, High-Functioning Autism, and Related Disorders*. Shawnee Mission, KS: Autism Asperger Publishing Company; www.asperger.net. Used with permission.

Get in Touch With What You Feel!!!

Scientific Name: Tactile

Special Talent: Helping your body decide what feels comfortable to you.

Preferred Habitat: Soft clothes, sometimes clothes that are loose, and sometimes clothes that are tight, foods that feel good in your mouth.

Potentially Unfriendly Environments: Clothes, food, art supplies, and personal grooming activities that make me feel more discomfort than I can tolerate.

You can help me if you ...: Try listening to the signals I send you, because it will give you clues on how to behave and keep you safe and comfortable.

From Moyer, S., NHS Inc. (2009). *The ECLIPSE Model: Teaching Self-Regulation, Executive Function, Attribution, and Sensory Awareness to Students with Asperger Syndrome, High-Functioning Autism, and Related Disorders.* Shawnee Mission, KS: Autism Asperger Publishing Company; www.asperger.net. Used with permission.

Touch Testing!

Tester Checklist

Items I Touched	Did I Like It?	Why or Why Not?

Getting to Know Myself: What Makes Me Happy, Sad, and Mad?

Directions: List at least three ideas for each column, if you can.

What Makes Me Happy?	What Makes Me Sad?	What Makes Me Mad?

HAMSTER

TURTLE

PARROT

MONKEY

GOAT

FROG

GUINEA PIG

CROW

SLOTH

DOG

CHICKEN

PIG

ZEBRA

BUFFALO

MOOSE

My Modulation Chart

How Serious Is It?	Situation	My First Response	A More Appropriate Response
1			
2			
3			

From Moyer, S., NHS Inc. (2009). *The ECLIPSE Model: Teaching Self-Regulation, Executive Function, Attribution, and Sensory Awareness to Students with Asperger Syndrome, High-Functioning Autism, and Related Disorders*. Shawnee Mission, KS: Autism Asperger Publishing Company; www.asperger.net. Used with permission.

My Modulation Chart

How Serious Is It?	Situation	My First Response	A More Appropriate Response
1			
2			
3			
4			
5			

From Moyer, S., NHS Inc. (2009). *The ECLIPSE Model: Teaching Self-Regulation, Executive Function, Attribution, and Sensory Awareness to Students with Asperger Syndrome, High-Functioning Autism, and Related Disorders*. Shawnee Mission, KS: Autism Asperger Publishing Company; www.asperger.net. Used with permission.

Balancing Situations and Strategies – Strategies

BRING NEXT TIME

ASK FOR HELP LOOKING

ASK WHAT TO EXPECT NEXT

BRING THINGS TO KEEP BUSY

SIT IN BACK OF ROOM

From Moyer, S., NHS Inc. (2009). *The ECLIPSE Model: Teaching Self-Regulation, Executive Function, Attribution, and Sensory Awareness to Students with Asperger Syndrome, High-Functioning Autism, and Related Disorders.* Shawnee Mission, KS: Autism Asperger Publishing Company; www.asperger.net. Used with permission.

Balancing Situations and Strategies – Strategies

TAKE BREAK

GET UP EARLIER

ASK WHAT THE RULES ARE

CALL VETERINARIAN

PLAY WITH SOMETHING ELSE

From Moyer, S., NHS Inc. (2009). *The ECLIPSE Model: Teaching Self-Regulation, Executive Function, Attribution, and Sensory Awareness to Students with Asperger Syndrome, High-Functioning Autism, and Related Disorders.* Shawnee Mission, KS: Autism Asperger Publishing Company; www.asperger.net. Used with permission.

Balancing Situations and Strategies – Situations

SUBSTITUTE TEACHER

LOSE VIDEO GAME

LOUD ASSEMBLY

CHANGE IN PLANS

LONG CAR RIDE

Balancing Situations and Strategies – Situations

MISS BUS

FIGHT WITH SIBLING

SICK PET

FORGET HOMEWORK

LOST TOY

Name That Goal!
Game Clues

1. My mom and I go to the grocery store after school once a week. I am stuck going, because Mom says that I am too young to stay home by myself. A lot of the time we end up in an argument because I don't want to stay with her the whole time. The truth is that I get tired of standing up so much and have a tough time not bumping into people around us in the aisles. **Possible answers: What is ... "Ask to sit down somewhere and wait, ask to push the cart so I can lean on it, or tell Mom it wears me out to follow her."**

2. When I am in gym class at school, the teacher blows her whistle and yells directions, but I am never sure if she is talking to me or not. Sometimes she gets angry at me because she says I didn't listen and makes me sit on the side. I wish I could be better at gym, but I can never tell what is going to happen next, and it makes me nervous, so I have trouble thinking fast enough. **Possible answers: What is ... "Ask the gym teacher to call my name when she needs me or stay close enough to the teacher to hear what she says."**

3. After school I like to play my video games because it gives me a chance to relax from all of the stuff I had to do at school. My mom wants me to do homework first, but when I try to do that, my brain feels like it's going to explode. Mom thinks I am trying to get out of doing my homework, but if I had time to relax first, I wouldn't mind doing it right before dinner. **Possible answers: What is ... "Explain that I just need to relax for a little while, pick a time to do my homework and DO IT, or tell Mom that my brain feels tired and as soon as I rest it gets better and I can do the work easily."**

4. Last week I got in trouble at school because I pushed a girl in the hallway. She made me mad, and I did it before I could think of anything else to do. The girl told me that I was "stupid" because I buy my lunch every day. I don't think it is stupid to buy lunch, because I really like the food. I didn't know what else to do, so I pushed her. **Possible answers: What is ... "Walk away, tell her to mind her own business, or tell a teacher."**

5. I usually like to have dinner with my family at holidays, but this time I had a meltdown. Dad and Grandma thought I was upset because they tried to make me eat more turkey, but that wasn't it at all. Grandma called me a "bad girl," and it made me angry. The truth is that I didn't want to sit at the table any more because my tights were making my legs itch. **Possible answers: What is ... "Explain that my tights are making me itch, ask politely to be excused, ask to take the tights off."**

From Moyer, S., NHS Inc. (2009). *The ECLIPSE Model: Teaching Self-Regulation, Executive Function, Attribution, and Sensory Awareness to Students with Asperger Syndrome, High-Functioning Autism, and Related Disorders.* Shawnee Mission, KS: Autism Asperger Publishing Company; www.asperger.net. Used with permission.

6. My brother and I were playing in the family room when he pushed the restart button on our video game. I grabbed his controller and threw it across the room, so he cried. My mom blamed me because I threw the controller, but I think she should have punished my brother. He only turns off the game when he is losing and wants to keep me from winning. **Possible answers: What is … "Not play video games with my brother, walk away instead of throwing the controller, or call Mom for help."**

7. There are so many books about Rome in our school library that I like to just sit on the floor and read them. The other day the librarian told my teacher I was disrespectful because I left a pile of books on the floor. Part of the problem was that I was so excited to read about Rome that I just kept looking for more information. I didn't want to put the books back in the wrong place, so I left them. **Possible answers: What is … "Take one book at a time and put it back before I get another, take one or two books to a table, or ask for help putting them back in the right place."**

8. My family went on a car trip last weekend to the state park. It was two hours away, and I got bored in the car. I kept asking how much longer it would be before we got there, and my parents got so angry that I wasn't allowed to hike my favorite trail when we finally got there. That punishment made no sense to me, because I always have trouble on long car rides, I can't stand sitting still that long. **Possible answers: What is … "Ask to bring toys, music, or books to keep me busy, bring a pillow and rest, or try to keep track of time so I know how much longer the trip will be."**

9. Every time we are in group and we go outside, I get in trouble because I would rather look at the bugs and things in nature than play the games we are supposed to be doing. The group leader says I have to stop. I get angry and sometimes yell at him. He says it is disrespectful not to do what he says, but I am not hurting anything. I just want to look for bugs. **Possible answers: What is … "Ask to split the time between the game and bug hunting, explain that playing group games outside makes me hot and sweaty, tell Mom or Dad that I need help resolving the problem."**

10. I got invited to a birthday party that included going to see a new cartoon movie. It was fun, but I got in trouble for not staying in my seat. They called my parents to come and get me. When my parents came, I got upset and cried because I wanted to stay with my friends. The problem was that the movie was so loud that I was getting a headache, and I thought if I left for a few minutes it would go away. **Possible answers: What is … "Don't go to the movies, but meet the group for the rest of the party, tell my friends that I am going to the bathroom because my head hurts, or hold my ears with my fingers for a while."**

From Moyer, S., NHS Inc. (2009). *The ECLIPSE Model: Teaching Self-Regulation, Executive Function, Attribution, and Sensory Awareness to Students with Asperger Syndrome, High-Functioning Autism, and Related Disorders.* Shawnee Mission, KS: Autism Asperger Publishing Company; www.asperger.net. Used with permission.

My Personal Modulation Tracker

Name: _____   Date: _____

Situation Number	How Serious Is It?	How Am I Responding?	Am I Balanced?
1			
2			
3			
4			
5			
6			
7			
8			
9			
10			

My Personal Modulation Tracker

Name: _____   Date: _____

Situation Number	How Serious Is It?	How Am I Responding?	Am I Balanced?
1			
2			
3			
4			
5			
6			
7			
8			
9			
10			

NOTES

NOTES

NOTES

AAPC

Autism Asperger Publishing Company
P.O. Box 23173
Shawnee Mission, Kansas 66283-0173
877-277-8254
www.asperger.net